D1744713

Derek Lewis

Where are you?

A Memoir

with thoughts on
God, Gravity and the Green Line

Grosvenor House
Publishing Limited

All rights reserved
Copyright © Derek Lewis, 2018

The right of Derek Lewis to be identified as the author of this
work has been asserted in accordance with Section 78
of the Copyright, Designs and Patents Act 1988

The book cover picture is copyright to Derek Lewis

This book is published by
Grosvenor House Publishing Ltd
Link House
140 The Broadway, Tolworth, Surrey, KT6 7HT.
www.grosvenorhousepublishing.co.uk

This book is sold subject to the conditions that it shall not, by way of
trade or otherwise, be lent, resold, hired out or otherwise circulated
without the author's or publisher's prior consent in any form of binding or
cover other than that in which it is published and
without a similar condition including this condition being imposed
on the subsequent purchaser.

A CIP record for this book
is available from the British Library

ISBN 978-1-78623-152-9

For
Ben, Sarah and Adam

In loving memory of your dear mother
Maple Karen Lewis (née Hayes-Richards)
1949–2005
and your dear sister
Miriam Leah Lewis 1976–2009

"May they be remembered for a blessing."

Contents

Volume 1

PREFACE

========

CONTENTS

Preface

My name, Derek, is a contraction of the German Theodoric meaning 'ruler of the people'. Since, however, I have not reached my full potential as a ruler of the people, and since my other achievements have been relatively modest, I came to the realisation that it is unlikely that anyone will write my biography. That being the case, I have set down some of my musings for posterity and hopefully in that way I might be remembered, if not for ruling the people, then for some level of human interest that may be conveyed in this process of self-indulgence.

The Rabbis of the Babylonian Talmud commented that it would be better not to have been born at all, but they go on to say that, since we are born, we should not turn away from experiencing pleasure in our lives because ultimately that is the reason why we have been put in this world. Of course at some point, the experience of pleasure comes to an end and then there is the inevitable let down. 'Too much laughter leads to tears', we were told by our parents. How right they were. Adults have the role of trying to understand and deal with many difficulties and even tragedies that may present in later life.

Strangely, there is a danger that dealing with those difficulties becomes confused with pleasure, because in the human spirit there is a quirk which lends a certain satisfaction and even pride in having 'broad shoulders'.

There is no real pleasure in the latter and it is probably a good idea to distinguish between the two.

Derek Lewis

Clerkenwell, January 2018

ROCK AROUND THE CLOCK

(Bill Hayley)

Looking back at my early life in Southend-on-Sea, I guess it was pretty idyllic. My maternal grandparents, were part of that desperate group of Jewish immigrants who had first fled the Cossacks and then extricated themselves from the teeming masses and sweatshops of London's East End to stake their claim to a fresh provincial life among the cockles and whelks of the Essex seaside.

My father's family also lived in the local area, so, as I grew up, I had many relatives at hand and most within walking distance of my house.

The town had a large Jewish population and whereas this certainly justified one orthodox synagogue, old habits die hard and there were two, so that the option existed for a disgruntled congregant to leave one synagogue in protest at some slight or injustice, and pray at the other.

In the earlier part of my childhood we lived in a nice detached house next door to the manager of the local Marks and Spencer, Manny Isaacs. The Jewish community was very proud that the manager of M & S was 'one of us' and we were proud to live next door to him.

From the age of about eight or nine years I walked by myself to the local primary school, dressed in short trousers come rain or snow, and I would happily skip along to school, sometimes picking and eating gooseberries from the hedge of the old house on the corner of

Kings Road. Then I would walk past Chalkwell Park (where that great Test cricketer Trevor Bailey played for Essex County) and into the quaint but prominent building which still, to this day, comprises Chalkwell Hall Junior School. I did not work all that hard at primary school but remember spending quite a lot of time playing kiss chase with the girls.

My parents both worked around the clock in my grandfather's clothing factory which was a provincial version of the sweatshop – more a perspiration shop, you might say.

Later my parents were in business on their own but, despite our apparent middle-class lifestyle, for various reasons they never really accumulated any assets and therefore, as I later realised, life was pretty much a hand to mouth existence.

They felt guilty about not having enough time to prepare a proper evening meal for me and to assuage their guilt they arranged for me to go, every day, to the Mayfair Buttery for lunch. This was a genteel dining establishment, not far from the school and, on the pretext of going home for lunch (school rule: eat at school or go home for lunch), I would nip around the corner to the diner, hang my school cap on the hat stand, and with a napkin carefully tucked in my collar, order three courses and put it 'on the account'. At nine years old this was good practice for what was to become the leitmotif of my later life viz, 1) eating in good restaurants, 2) breaking establishment rules, and 3) living beyond my means.

After school, as the proverbial latch key kid, I would go home, make myself a jam sandwich and listen to the little Ekco wireless set in the morning room or watch the TV which showed life as it really was in those days – black and white.

The wireless was plastic, then a fashionable new material that followed Bakelite, and it had an aerial wire protruding from the back which could be moved in various directions to encourage better reception. I had an inquiring mind as a child but my curiosity was tempered, on one particular occasion when, attempting to get a better reception, I stuffed the aerial wire into the mains electricity.

Fortunately I survived but I will not disguise the fact that this was a slight set back to my aspirations of a career in science.

I had a brother, but did not see that much of him. He was eight years older than me and went on the train to London every day. He was supposed to be going to the London College of Fashion, but apparently bunked off most of the time pursuing nefarious activities such as boating in Regent's Park. Until my dad found out. That was my first observation of harsh parental discipline which I found fascinating – my brother was less enamoured.

When I was twelve years old, I lost half of my brother. This was the result of my parents informing me that my mother had, in fact, been divorced before she met my father and that my brother was the product of the previous marriage.

It seems that they had wanted to save the news until I was really able to appreciate the shock.

A divorce was pretty unusual in those days and explained a lot, especially why my brother was tall dark and handsome, while the rest of us were well, none of the above, a fact that a friend later told me, that everyone in the local community had noticed, with the exception of me.

Also, he was named Tony, I assume after an award.

Unlike me, he was never mistaken for an oil rig.

I went to Hebrew classes three times a week. On those days I had to wear the traditional fringed undergarment which signifies that a boy is of the Hebrew persuasion. At school, when changing for PE classes, I would desperately try to conceal these fringes from my school friends, but often to no avail. The acute embarrassment and teasing that followed as my classmates found out the secret of my undergarments, never quite left me, but it was good grounding for future life as a member of a religious minority.

He's Got The Whole World In His Hands

(Laurie London)

What sort of present do you buy for a Bar Mitzvah boy who has just become a man? If you are invited to the dinner and dance, maybe a pen, or a watch but usually it's just easier to write a cheque.

After the recitation of my portion in the synagogue a lavish party was to be held at the Westward Ho Hotel on the Sunday. Some of the guests were barely known to me as many were distant relatives of my parents but their names slowly unfolded with the cheques that were received prior to the big day.

Considering the 'religious' nature of the event you may consider it a little hypocritical to judge people by their gifts, but a 'black tie' event at the Westward Ho cost bucks and appraising the presents appealed to the baser instincts. To put it into context, in 1960, a cheque in the sum of say five guineas as a gift was considered about right. A guinea was one pound (sterling) plus one shilling and such a gesture had to be in guineas. This was probably because the guinea was the monetary unit charged by lawyers and doctors at the time for their services, and we were, after all, providing a service.

A cheque duly arrived from my father's cousin, Willy and his wife Tilly London. It was for three guineas. You will not be surprised to know that London was not their original Russian name.

Willy and Tilly ran a dry-cleaning shop and I knew who they were, because their son Laurie London had achieved world fame a couple of years earlier with his recording *He's Got The Whole World In His Hands.*

You may come to the conclusion that this contribution of three guineas was a tad on the low side bearing in mind that their son was, at that time, No 2 in the American hit parade, but it was, nevertheless, gratefully received.

The Sunday evening arrived and in those days, after dinner, Jewish middle-class convention dictated that the Bar Mitzvah boy danced a waltz with his mother. My mother, who was a talented designer, had made herself a fabulous red satin flamenco dress and so, eschewing prevailing custom, I danced the cha cha with her to open the dancing.

Later, Willy London came up to me, slapped me on the back and with a hearty 'mazeltov' handed me an envelope.

Upon checking the contents of the envelope (in a toilet cubicle by the way) I found that the envelope contained £150.

To get a grasp of how much that would be in today's money you would have to multiply the amount by at least twenty times so in today's money it would be roughly £3,000.

An uncle of mine much later told me I was lucky I was in the toilet!

When I told him, my father thought I had been hallucinating until I dragged him to the restrooms. He checked with Willy, who said yes, it was for me and he was happy that I was happy and he was happy that my father was happy and that we should all have good health and be happy.

Great story eh, rich second cousin decides to help out poor long lost relative?

Well so it appeared, at least until midnight when we received a desperate telephone call from Tilly London to say that Willy had accidentally given me the week's takings from the dry-cleaning shop which she had handed to him in the car for safe keeping. He, not realising that she had previously sent me a cheque for three guineas, assumed it was my present.

We returned the money. The box of chocolates we received from them was nice.

'My Bar Mitzvah 1960'

Shakin' All Over

(Johnny Kidd and the Pirates)

My secondary school was Westcliff High School for Boys. It was a Church of England state grammar school of one thousand boys which, in those days, thought itself a public school, that peculiarly English institution of rugby and floggings.

We were short of neither. In fact it was the rugby coach who performed many of the floggings and these had to be inflicted on a bared bottom. One of my old school mates pointed out to me years later (he was a physician at Southend General Hospital) that the old rugby master, would, these days, have been put in prison for such activities. I had never thought that much about it until he mentioned it. Maybe he had to bare his bottom more often than me.

The school premises were built in 1926 and included surrounding grounds and sports fields. By the time I had arrived they also comprised squash courts and a swimming pool. We were ruled over by Masters, who patrolled the quadrangles wearing cloaks and often mortar boards. They looked like early day versions of Darth Vader, with canes instead of light sabres.

The Jews and Catholics in the school numbered about forty or fifty. As a rule, each group had separate religious services in the morning and after the Jews finished declaring 'Hear O'Israel' and the Catholics had said their 'Hail Marys', both groups would line up outside the main assembly hall preparing to enter for the school notices. At the appropriate time the prefects were instructed to 'call in the dissenters', which, if you did not know, is the collective name for a group of Jews and Catholics.

Actually, I was not bothered about being called a dissenter, because by this time, my well developed sense of paranoia almost seemed to justify this quasi celebrity status and, as long as I could avoid getting my head bashed in by a non dissenter, then being called one seemed, in a strange way, worthwhile.

On the last day of term, 1963, however, there were no separate services, as full attendance at assembly was mandatory for all boys, on this most significant of days.

As prayers commenced we, of the persuasion, self consciously shuffled on our feet looking over our shoulders to see if the voices of a thousand C of Es, invoking 'Our Father, Who art in Heaven' was actually having any effect.

I should explain that the sixth form school leavers each year traditionally played some kind of sensational leaving prank during their last few days in school but, so far, we had seen nothing.

Previous years had, for instance, seen such inventive ruses as the overnight appearance of giant footprints up the walls of the school or peashooter snipers hidden in the roof void of the main hall using the masters as targets. One year a yacht, belonging to one of the masters, appeared in the swimming pool.

On this day of days, which is forever etched in my memory, the headmaster, otherwise known as 'The Boot' was ensconced in the centre of the rostrum on his throne with masters in full regalia at the back of the hall facing him. As was customary the Lesson from the Bible was then read by one of the prefects standing to the right of the headmaster with the head boy standing to the left.

The reading of the day was the Parable of the Dry Bones from Ezekiel and the prefect, in a suitably grave voice, intoned... *"Dry bones, hear the word of the LORD! This is what the LORD says to these bones: I will make breath enter you, and you will come to life..."*

Right on cue, as if controlled by some spiritual force, the curtains behind the headmaster parted and, as the jaws of a thousand boys dropped open, a full sized skeleton (from the science lab) hovered behind The Boot, swinging to and fro... *"and as I prophesied, there was a rattling sound, and the bones came together, bone to bone..."*

The Boot could not see, but the head boy could and tried to cover up the prank. He leaned over and pulled the curtains. He tugged... it rattled, he tugged again... and it was shakin' all over. The masters facing forward and confronted by this horror, rushed out of the room and down the side of the quadrangles, a phalanx of Darth Vaders ready to exorcise the Force.

The more the head boy tugged, the more the skeleton shook, and finally, unable to control themselves, a thousand boys collapsed into hysterics...

WALK LIKE A MAN

(Frankie Valli and the Four Seasons)

Having completed the mandatory part of my secondary education, the thought of going on to further education had been anathema to me, so I left school.

In those days only really clever kids stayed on to take A Levels and less than 5% of the country's school population went on to university. Therefore, armed with my General Certificate of Education in mathematics (Distinction), english (language and literature), physics and art, I had left Westcliff High School for Boys for ever. Freedom, hurrah!

After enjoying the usual school holiday of six weeks I was shocked when my father told me that I was required to find a job or choose a career.

In those days a middle-class Jewish boy, with any sort of brain had a pretty clear choice. Unless he went to work for his parents (in my case the rag trade, so forget it) he could become a solicitor, an accountant or even worse an estate agent.

The latter seemed the best option to me because I imagined that the two former jobs involved sitting behind a desk all day whereas an estate agent would at least have some freedom to muck about. Also a friend of my brother's had qualified as a chartered surveyor and was, by all accounts, doing very well working in London in commercial property. That seemed to be the best choice.

Accordingly, I joined the Chartered Institute of Auctioneers and Estate Agents as a student member, and went to look for a job.

In those days you had to learn your trade from the bottom rung of the ladder.

I went for an interview with Knight Frank & Rutley for the position of tea boy. When I did not get offered the job I learned an important lesson in life, which was that there were people out there who did not necessarily judge you on your skills. I realised this because, after all, I could make tea!

I wandered around the West End of London for a week or two, going into various estate offices and asking if they needed an office junior, and finally I was offered a position at West End agency, Brecker Grossmith. My wages were four pounds and ten shillings per week.

My career had started.

At Brecker Grossmith, in 1963, I was one of two office juniors and basically our jobs consisted of making coffee in the morning, and tea in the afternoon for all the staff and other general duties including printing, photocopying, stuffing envelopes and manning the telephone switchboard at lunchtime. We were housed in the basement of the shop premises in Wigmore Street.

Printing was done on a Gestetner duplicating machine and our job consisted of placing a waxed stencil on the machine (which had previously been typed by a secretary), squeezing copious amounts of black ink into a special slot and then switching on the printer (believe it or not we had electricity in those days). The roller then revolved around, printing the requisite details on paper while at the same time liberally spraying the office juniors with ink.

The Gestetner printing machine was one of the most sophisticated and successful pieces of office equipment at the time. Years later I learned that after the war the Gestetner brothers had approached my grandfather, who had a factory in Pitfield Street, Hoxton, to offer him a partnership in their new invention which subsequently was to become ubiquitous in the business world. Unfortunately he passed on the opportunity which probably accounts for why I was only left £50 in my grandfather's will.

The other modern piece of equipment that I learned to use as an office junior was a photocopying machine. I urge you not to confuse the term 'photocopying machine' with the plain paper copier of today. This sublime piece of equipment comprised a metal tray which contained a liquid with various rollers attached. In order to reproduce say, a single letter, the original needed to be introduced into a roller together with some photographic paper both of which would be fed into the machine and the two pieces of paper having been through the liquid would appear at the end of the tray stuck together. When the photographic paper was peeled away, a copy of the original miraculously appeared. Both pieces of paper would need to be set aside to dry.

When our dedicated switchboard operator went for lunch, one of the juniors would be allowed up from the basement and required to operate the 'dolls eye' switchboard which had 10 incoming telephone lines and 15 extensions and was situated by the front door of the shop. This required wearing heavy Bakelite carbon headphones, and when a call came in, it was necessary to pull out a plug with a lead on it, pulling a lever to signal the extension that you would be calling. When the dolls eye winked, the plug could be inserted in the appropriate hole and the connection made.

After three months, two negotiators who dealt with small West End offices left the company and the other junior, Philip, and I were instructed to sit at their desks and 'hold the fort'.

Philip did not enjoy this, as he preferred to continue getting sprayed with ink in the basement. For me it was a game changer and within a week or so, I had agreed my first deal, which was the letting of a small office suite of 500sq ft to an American businessman, who did not seem fazed when he visited the offices, only to find me wearing headphones and being winked at by miscellaneous doll's eyes.

Time to move on.

My next job was as a junior negotiator at Barnett Baker & Co. Denys Barnett and Ralph Baker ran their commercial agency with their secretary. I was doing the junior stuff and also earning commission on various deals that I was encouraged to negotiate. It was a great learning curve.

We shared our offices in Hanover Square, Mayfair with Perthpoint Investments and the Hurst Park Syndicate, who were also our clients. Perthpoint was run by Jarvis Astaire who went on to become the owner of Wembley Stadium and Hurst Park was run by Sam Burns who was the manager of Terry Downes, World Middleweight Boxing Champion of 1961. Sam's son John was to become the Chairman of Derwent London one of the largest property companies in London with assets of over £3.4bn.

After two and a half years at Barnett Baker I accepted a job with Kenneth Brown & Company as a fully fledged negotiator earning £10 per week and 10% commission on deals that I put through. I worked with my colleague, Michael Freedman, and we ran the West End Offices department of the company.

Michael and I shared an office and a secretary and had our names painted on the door. I was seventeen.

We shared a glazed partition with one of the associate partners, Neil Sinclair, and got up to various schoolboy antics including making faces at Neil through the partition so that he could not stop grinning when he was interviewing clients. We often threw darts at each other during the day. Michael grew his hair very long.

I was fired after 10 months and Mike followed shortly thereafter.

No Particular Place To Go

(Chuck Berry)

'The Square' was an open concrete bastion projecting out into the sea like the prow of some beached cruise ship. On summer days like this, the grass patch in the middle would be covered in striped deckchairs where the older girls, that is to say the ones in their mid-twenties, would be set to roast in their bikinis, basting themselves with Ambre Solaire.

The older guys, that is my brother's contemporaries, would sometimes show off by diving into the sea from the bastion walls when the tide was in, and I had even done this myself a few times although the game was more about 'hanging out', than swimming.

Bondi Beach it wasn't. Still, occasionally, when it was exceptionally hot we would swim and play water polo just next to The Square.

Years later my brother told me that the water company pumped raw sewage into the sea right there, but these things seemed to be of little concern in the mid-1960s and we seemed to have survived.

On this particular Sunday, my eyes were a bit sore after the previous late night, the effect of my newfangled contact lenses, which had replaced the spectacles that I had been wearing since the age of ten.

The wraparound sunglasses seemed to do the trick and also looked cool. My friend, Andy, drove up in his Aston Martin DB5 which he had received the previous year from his father as a seventeenth birthday present. I hopped in.

My dad's Ford Cortina was never available on a Sunday, although I did have the use of the Bedford 15cwt van from the factory, but it did not exactly compare to the DB5 as a 'pulling' vehicle.

We checked out the cafés under the arches and Rossi's Ice Cream parlour (still there today) and, satisfied that we were not missing out in Westcliff, heading over to the centre of Southend.

Five minutes later, with a quick double de-clutch and a low growl up Pier Hill we turned into Royal Terrace.

This quiet Regency street contained a parade of genteel guesthouses overlooking the Estuary including the Naval and Military Club and also, somewhat incongruously, the Shrubbery coffee bar.

The Shrubbery was the cool local hang-out carved from the ground floor of the last house on the street.

We cruised past.

It was de rigueur to do a couple of circuits around the block before entering, in order to impress anyone standing outside. The actual number of circuits was somewhat dependent on whether there were any other poseurs around, say Pete with his yellow E-Type Jag, or Tony with his Crayford converted Corsair. If you were not careful they could really steal your thunder.

Fortunately, on this occasion we hit the jackpot. We had arrived early so there were no other contenders and, as luck would have it, there were two new girls, a brunette and a blonde, sitting on the low wall outside.

They were from slightly out of town, and were drinking Cokes and smiling as the muffled sound of

Chuck Berry emanated from the juke box inside '...no particular place to go...'

These were the sixties, two guys, an Aston Martin DB5, wraparound sunglasses, a blonde and a brunette. Life did not get much better.

SHE WAS ONLY SIXTEEN

(Craig Douglas)

It was Sunday, a balmy summer's day in 1964, and she was sitting alone on the low wall outside the Shrubbery coffee bar gazing lazily over the cliffs and the Thames Estuary. She was only sixteen, a striking girl with more than a hint of oriental features, in a blue top, ski pants and black ballet pumps.

Andy and I had double-dated the girl and her friend once before and I remembered that she was studying at a dance school in Romford.

On that previous occasion I had drawn the blonde, and, in truth, had been disappointed, because the brunette was the real beauty. Since, however, Andy had been playing Sean Connery in the Aston Martin at the time, and I was just shotgun, I could hardly complain.

Fortunately, on this particular weekend, Andy was in hot pursuit of one of the dancers at the Cliffs Pavilion, so despite the inconvenience of being without the DB5, I had my opportunity.

We arranged to have lunch the following week, in London.

Later, she told me that the only other times she had been to London was to buy ballet shoes from Anello & Davide in Covent Garden.

Nowadays, it is a bit difficult to understand how exotic this girl was in 1964. Her father had fought in the Burma campaign and had come back home with a stunning Burmese wife. The girl had inherited the most wonderful almond eyes and a fantastic smile. I was smitten.

She came up to London and we had lunch, alfresco, at the Lantern Bistro on the corner of Duke Street and Wigmore Street.

I had taken the afternoon off work and after lunch, we walked arm in arm down Bond Street, window shopping. Later, I travelled back with her from Fenchurch Street to her station and we kissed on the train.

Although inseparable for the next year or so, we were much too young to consider anything more permanent. She left dance school and started her first summer season in Hastings. The relationship started to ebb and our last official date was dinner at the Hilton Rooftop Restaurant on her eighteenth birthday.

Six months went by and although we did get together again trying to catch the harmony of that first love, she had outgrown me. By that time she was dancing at a famous club called the Latin Quarter in the West End and was seeing the drummer of the club's band.

I bumped into her many years later, in a coffee shop just off Hanover Square. We spoke briefly. She was still as beautiful as ever and happily married to the drummer with a family...

Hatikvah

(National Anthem of Israel)

Looking back to 1967 when I was 19 years old, I cannot believe how little I understood about Israel's precarious position in the world. To me Israel was just a distant foreign land with many poor Jewish immigrants, and although my father would regularly hand over a ten shilling note to the 'blue box' collector and occasionally my parents would pack up some old clothes 'for Israel', I had not thought of the place as special. We had certainly never been there. The money was for the Jewish National Fund and the Joint Palestine Appeal because, in fact, Jews, among others, were the Palestinians of the time.

Then, as the tension escalated, suddenly it hit me – this place was part of me and for some unaccountable reason the whole Arab world was poised to destroy it and kill 'my family'. Thousands of us gathered outside the Jewish Agency building at Rex House to volunteer and in a week or so, huddled together in an old Bristol Britannia aircraft I, and my group, flew by night and landed at Lod airport...

Strange to think that this was the beginning of my love affair with Israel and that six years later I would be living there, studying, working and bringing up a young family.

To those who are interested in my story, they will not begin to understand me if they do not understand my feelings about Israel.

Israel's stunning victory in the Six-Day War was as much a shock to most Western European governments as it was to the defeated Arab nations. Israel was now no longer a beleaguered nation or an underdog, and, while the Europeans had purported a level of sympathy towards Israel prior to 1967, they gradually began to change their perspective and resent Israel's successes.

The problems that exist between the Jew and his Arab cousins are historical, biblical and educational and are not for this book but they are fuelled by the attitude of many who, in truth, are unable to see Jews as anything other than victims.

A recent exchange with a sceptic on Facebook, will demonstrate my position:

The Comment

"Honestly there is a lot that Israel could do to redeem its image on the world. Maybe then I could consider standing with Israel. There aren't many nations in the world that expand every year by taking more and more land from their neighbours. Nor do most countries cut their neighbours land up with a huge wall. Sorry… I'm pro Jew and pro 1967 borders, but anti-settlement and anti-apartheid."

My Reply

"Dear…,

You think you are 'pro Jew', but in truth you are 'pro Jew as a victim'. As soon as the Jew erects a wall to protect himself from being blown up, slaughtered or otherwise murdered, you come out with the old canard of 'apartheid' and loaded references to the '1967 lines'.

There are 1.5m Arabs living in Israel who have one man one vote, who are represented by duly elected political parties and have all the freedoms of any Israeli citizen. Meanwhile, there are 300m Arabs living in 22 sovereign states worldwide, all of whom would give their right arm to live under the freedoms enjoyed by the Israeli Arab... that is assuming they have not lost their right arm because they stole a loaf of bread!

When you refer to the 1967 lines, you are referring to that area that was occupied by Jordan in 1948 (you know... that country that consists of 76% of Mandated Palestine, and where 60% of the population are Palestinian Arabs), at which time all the Jews were kicked out of Jerusalem, their religious sites desecrated and the Holy City was made 'Judenrein' for the first time in 2000 years.

Jordan's occupation, of course, was never internationally recognized at the time, even by the Arab League and therefore the 1967 'lines' are by no means set in stone. So, while it is really sad to hear when affluent 'do gooders' cannot resist the propaganda of the liberal left, when push comes to shove, I will happily go to the trenches with... to defend Israel, just as we did in 1967..."

and,

"...Sorry, but I feel bound to reply, if just to set the record straight regarding these 'insightful Jewish academics' you quote: Klug and Chomsky.

Please do not be swayed by the politics of these so called 'academics' – even if they are Jewish.

These two characters are well known as being up their own fundaments. Klug effectively denies Israel's right to exist (as if Israel needs his permission) and Chomsky is a self-proclaimed anarchist (so, as far as your investment in Chomsky's film, I would say that your money could have been put to better use).

The link you sent me to Klug's article ('No, anti-Zionism is not anti-Semitism') is very telling if not for any other reason than it highlights the phenomenon of the self-hating Jew.

Firstly, he claims that many Jews resisted the aspirations of Zionism in 1897... of course they did! They were terrified that the nations of the world would view the claim to have a modern nation state as an outrageous audacity, precisely because they felt that the natural place in the world for the Jew at that time was to be bent in obeisance and available for the usual persecution.

He then goes on to suggest that nationalism, specifically in Palestine was irrelevant to the Jews who just wanted a safe haven after centuries of just such persecution. This is demonstrably not true because at different times the Jews were offered a number of alternative places as a homeland including, inter alia, parts of Argentina, Uganda and indeed Russia.

All of these were rejected in favor of the area known, by the way, for the previous 400 years as the Ottoman Province of Southern Syria, an area of land over which no Arab nation had ever claimed sovereignty and over which the only people who had ever exercised national and historic sovereignty were – the Jews.

The British Foreign Secretary, Lord Balfour understood all this in 1917 because he read the Bible, and for anyone who reads the Bible, even if they are not religious but merely regard is as a quasi historical document for children, it is still pretty clear that the Jews are connected to the area.

It is quite extraordinary, that human rights activists in the West did not bat an eyelid when the government of Sri Lanka killed 20,000 civilians in the final push against the Tamil Tigers a couple of years ago, and yet somehow they find that they cannot sleep at night over the fact that it may take a Palestinian Arab an hour to cross an Israeli checkpoint to work (or maybe set off a bomb) and therefore feel the compulsion to lobby for boycott, divestment and sanctions against the only free, democratic and pluralist nation in the Middle East..."

and,

"...No problem, happy to clarify and it's good to know that there are people who are prepared to listen.

Meanwhile, I hope you do not think I am ducking the settlements' issue, so maybe I can just conclude by demonstrating that the settlements are really not the obstacle to peace.

There are three categories of settlements; 1) suburban population growth over the green line, 2) security settlements in the Jordan Valley, and 3) settlements in Judea and Samaria.

The solutions to these three categories are well understood by both parties. The first can be resolved by a mutually agreed exchange of land and the second will not be retained after security confidence has been established.

As regards the third category, these settlements, are built on land that has been appropriated under Ottoman Law, which is actually the relevant legal system in the area.

Ideally, of course, the proposed Palestinian State will not wish to be completely 'Judenrein' and they will accept, say, a quota of Jews as citizens, but in any event, it is important to note that it is not impossible to remove these settlements, as indeed Israel has proved by previous examples in Sinai and Gaza. Desperately traumatic… but not impossible.

So, the problem then, is not the settlements.

Furthermore, the current administration is not the problem, because it is famously the right wing governments that succeed in these matters, as demonstrated in the case of Menachem Begin's peace deal with Egypt's Sadat and indeed Ariel Sharons's unilateral withdrawal from Gaza.

Notably, previous left wing governments have failed dismally, even after making 'pip squeaking' concessions and offering 95% of everything demanded by the PA.

No, there is only one obstacle to peace and that is the insistence by the Palestinian Arabs of the return of 2m 'refugees' which includes the descendants of around only 500,000 Arabs that left Israel in 1948, somewhat less than the 700,000 Jews that had to leave the Arab countries as the result of the War of Independence."

'At the River Jordan 1967'

Under African Skies

(Paul Simon)

Somewhere off the coast of West Africa, before Las Palmas, all the passengers came out on deck. Maple leaned forward against the rail of the Pendennis Castle and watched as the RMS *Arundel Castle* passed them about half a mile away.

The purser had explained at dinner the night before that the following morning their sister, ship RMS *Arundel*, would be seen on the starboard side heading for the Cape and, since both ships had embarked on Thursday from their respective ports, when they passed at sea that was the midpoint of the journey.

The purser hosted a table at dinner each night in tourist class for the few that were travelling alone, much as the captain hosted dinner in first class. John was in his mid-thirties and always looked smart in his starched white shirt with the stitched gold epaulettes.

The ships blew their horns, siblings acknowledging each other. The passengers chattered excitedly and waved as the Arundel grew first larger, then smaller. In a few days the RMS *Pendennis Castle* would arrive at Southampton.

It was Susan's father who had suggested that Maple might consider going to England by ship. Susan was Maple's friend. They had worked together selling wigs at Coulson's Department Store in Cape Town and Maple had spent Christmas at Susan's house.

This was quite a big deal as Susan's dad was none other than the American ambassador to South Africa, William Manning Rountree.

Over Christmas dinner he had mentioned that a Union Castle mail ship left Cape Town every week for England but also carried passengers and he thought it was cheaper than flying. He was right, at least if you shared a cabin in tourist class, and this Maple did, with a young lady who had been visiting her mother and was now on her way back to her husband and little girl in Surrey.

In Cape Town Maple had spent quite a lot of time talking to her uncle David and after the latest little chat she now understood why the family had not objected to her spending Christmas with Susan's family. They did not seem to celebrate Christmas and were happy that she had found a family to be with.

She had known that her mother was Jewish of course, but her uncle seemed insistent that this meant that Maple was also Jewish and hinted that she might wish to consider living a more Jewish life, whatever that meant. She thought this a pretty weird suggestion, being as she considered herself an Anglican, if anything, and she was certainly not ready to give up Christmas.

She really liked her uncle David and tried to comprehend his point of view, but the lifestyle he was talking about sounded very strange and restrictive and anyway she had enough trouble adjusting to apartheid South Africa let alone a new religion. As it was she could not get used to the fact that a black man, old enough to be her grandfather was called 'the boy' and had served her breakfast in bed every morning.

Anyway she was quite looking forward to spending a couple of weeks meeting the English side of the family and then finally returning home to Canada, and of course Steve. It was sooner than intended but Steve missed her and she knew he missed her because he had sent her a BOAC flight ticket from England back to Canada.

South Africa had certainly been a learning curve. Maple mused on her previously sheltered existence in Canada casting her mind back to school at Crystal Beach, then South London Collegiate and finally Fanshawe College where she did a vocational course in hairdressing.

She had apprenticed at a hairdressing salon but until this trip, nothing very exciting had happened in her life except that the proprietor's wife had tried to get Maple to spy on her husband who apparently was having an affair with one of the customers. She balked at this which had not done much for her career.

She had not been an academic success like her sister. Rather, she was athletic and had been junior champion at the Ontario Conference Meet and senior basketball champion at the 1964 Western Ontario Secondary School games four years earlier. She had only been fifteen at the time but, although her achievements had reached the local newspapers, this did not seem to count for much in the real world. On the plus side she was slim, skinny even, and a pretty girl, at least Steve thought so.

Maple had been born the year after her parents had come to Canada from England. She knew that her mother was from a large immigrant family in the East End of London, England, and that her mother's family originally came from somewhere in Russia.

In Crystal Beach, life had not been easy for her parents, what with her mom slaving in the restaurant and dad away so much selling sidings or medical books. Larry, her brother, had left and was in Cyprus with the UN forces and her sister had just married and moved to Northern Ontario.

She now lived in London, Ontario which was respectably close to Toronto but since she was the only one left at home, she had gotten engaged to Steve. It seemed the obvious thing to do as she was pretty sure she loved Steve. Well, they had been together for two years.

Since she was only nineteen, her parents were not happy about the engagement, particularly her dad who had just forked out a small fortune for her sister's wedding, which he had to borrow from the bank.

Then, seemingly out of the blue, she had been invited to visit her mother's sister in South Africa. The deal was, that she was to stay with her aunt and uncle, work in South Africa for a year and then, when she returned, if she still wanted to marry Steve, her parents would give their blessing.

She agreed to the deal and there was much crying and buying of crimplene dresses and matching luggage. That was six months earlier and she had left, with a thousand dollars in her new plastic wallet, wearing the diamond engagement ring that Steve had bought her.

It was now Wednesday and it had been six days since they had seen the HMS *Arundel*. She had spent most of the day playing bingo or in the games room as it was becoming chilly outside during the day and she had stopped sunbathing a while back. Two young Belgian brothers had challenged her to table tennis and were quite embarrassed that neither could get the better of her even though they had been playing for hours.

Dinner that evening was good fun. They had all gotten a bit merry with champagne as they celebrated their last night at sea.

Around ten thirty, Maple went back to the cabin, changed into her pyjamas and climbed up to the top bunk. Her roommate, whom she had last seen in the bar with a large martini had not come back yet. so she turned on her transistor radio to see if she could find some music. This had been futile for the last week but after fiddling with the tuner knob she found a station in English called Radio Luxembourg and snuggled up to listen to the American top thirty.

As the station faded in and out she heard the disc jockey's snatched news references to Vietnam war protests, student revolution in France and some guy in New York named Kornfeld who was planning a big concert in a place called Woodstock. She picked up her Harold Robbins book and read the final pages whilst she listened to the music. Jason Cord the hero had just rushed to the bedside of his only love Rina Marlowe. She drifted off.

The huge ginger tom crouched ready to pounce as the mouse was walking backwards to the corner of the room, desperately looking over it's shoulder for a hole in the skirting board. Maple's eyes opened as the little creature squealed...

The room was dark apart from the subdued light of the outside deck lamp and she could just make out her roommate sitting in the chair by the door with her head back, was it her making that sound? Then the faint light caught the flash of a gold epaulette on a white shirt and Maple's jaw dropped as reality dawned on her.

Her heart pounded and, snapping her eyes shut, she turned over as quietly as she could and tried to recall each of the top thirty in reverse order.

The next day there was a brief goodbye hug as they disembarked at Southampton and Maple watched as her roommate ran into the arms of her husband at the dockside.

Uncle Alec, a small stocky man and one of her mother's brothers (and my father), was waiting for her, and they drove from the port to the east coast of England to meet the rest of the family.

She would never get to return to Cape Town but many years later she would be drawn to the magical harmony of Paul Simon and the Soweto Choir which always reminded her of her time in Africa.

Aquarius

(Cast of Hair)

The swinging sixties were coming to a close and in England the psychedelic era beckoned, having started, more or less, the year before in the USA as epitomised in Tom Wolfe's classic book the *Electric Kool-Aid Acid Test*.

I was at that time working as a commercial property agent for Henry Berney & Co., Surveyors, of Regent Street and sharing a flat in Bayswater with my friend Russell and his two sisters. Russell was assistant to the famous hairdresser Vidal Sassoon and worked at Vidal's iconic salon in Old Bond Street.

Socially, life revolved around friends from Southend some of whom lived in London but often as not, I would spend the weekends back home, staying with my parents.

My career had been slightly held back by the fact that in June 1967, I had volunteered to go to Israel at the start of what was to become known as the 'Six-Day War'.

Fortunately, I had returned in one piece by November of that year and, all in all, by the beginning of 1969, I was doing okay as a negotiator although, it has to be said, my enthusiasm for the job was waning.

On the romantic front I had split up with my first real girlfriend three years earlier. We had been together for almost two years, but being so young and from such different backgrounds we both knew that the relationship was not going anywhere. Looking back, had we been a couple of years older things might have turned out differently, although boy, it would have taken all my negotiating skills to settle the Anglo-Burmese/Jewish question! Still we both moved on.

I had a few more girlfriends during the next couple of years but not a big roll call in the scheme of things.

Working in the West End, I would often go to lunch at a Hungarian restaurant just off Bond Street. The food was pretty good but the real attraction was the waitress who I later found out was the proprietor's daughter. We would see each other quite often, but the petite blonde was looking for a husband and I was not serious enough!

For a few months after that I went out with a secretary who worked for the Israeli shipping company, Zim. She was a beautiful girl and a great romantic, but she had never really gotten over her very first boyfriend and frankly no one else measured up.

In Israel, in 1967, I had met the proverbial 'all American girl', a psychology major from Berkeley (University of California). She followed me back to England after I left Israel but, although we spent a lot of time together, we were never kindred spirits.

Then there was my sophisticated phase with a girl who was assistant to one of the directors of the famous publishers W H Allen. She had been at the sister secondary school to ours and her previous boyfriend, whom I knew pretty well, was later to become one of the UK's biggest impresarios. I am not sure that he ever quite forgave me for taking her out after they split up, but ironically he later became a big client of mine. She and I would often go to the theatre and dine out but although she was great company there was no real chemistry between us.

By 1968 I was renting a large Queen Anne property in North London called The Ivy House, which I shared with four other housemates. It was a rambunctious party house. My girlfriend at the time was a beautiful hometown girl, great fun and she even had the privilege of meeting my parents, but once again this did not evolve into anything serious!

The age of Aquarius was coming to an end and, lovely as they all were, settling down was far from my mind.

Lucy In The Sky
With Diamonds

(The Beatles)

I am not sure of the qualities needed for someone to be considered a best mate, but I think that lending ten shillings to your friend on a Saturday night to keep him going for the week is pretty much up there as one of those qualities, so Bernie certainly fitted the profile, as I was the recipient.

Bernie and I had become firm friends during our early years and, although we went to different secondary schools we had met at Hebrew classes which we attended three times a week and had spent a lot of time hanging out together at the local Jewish youth club.

By the age of 17 our horizons were broadening and we were frequenting the cool Southend-on-Sea hotspots, such the Shrubbery Coffee Bar and, the forbidden (by our parents), Studio Jazz Club, which hosted many of the iconic music stars of that era, including John Lee Hooker, Keith Richards, Georgie Fame, Donovan, and Procol Harum, among many others.

On Saturday nights we would often play poker with our mates, unless, of course, one of us was dating. We played a lot of poker.

One of our aspirations as best mates was to go on holiday together to an exotic place, and a couple of years later we booked to go to Ibiza for the holiday of a lifetime.

And so it was that Bernard and myself arrived at our hotel in Talamanca Bay in the summer of 1970 and it did not disappoint. I did not know it at the time, but this was to be my last holiday as a single guy.

While in Ibiza we had gone to visit some friends, two brothers, who were staying on Formentera which is one of the smaller Balearic Islands next to Ibiza. We had spent the morning sitting on the beach admiring the girls. The sun was very hot and when cold glasses of lime juice appeared out of nowhere we were very grateful.

It had been two years since Tom Wolfe had published the *Electric Kool-Aid Acid Test*...

Some would say that spiking a person's drink with acid is a touch outrageous, and many would strongly hold that position but the experience was certainly a profound one and the fact remains that our friends chaperoned us carefully, so just as there is honour amongst thieves, apparently, there is also honour amongst psychedelic drug users.

Pretty soon I noticed that my vision had become ultra sensitive and I was starting to hallucinate. Having smoked quite a lot of marijuana and heard a lot about LSD, I was aware that at all times I had to keep my mind focused on pleasant thoughts, not that difficult on a Spanish beach with the sun, the sea and the view of beautiful girls.

Bernard was tall, dark with long black hair and had taken to wearing a large wooden cross around his neck. He strode off up a mountain, and we followed. Several hours later, during the passage of which the necessity of minutely examining various plants and flowers took on an overpowering significance, we arrived at a lake.

I say lake, but it was, of course, the lagoon of paradise.

I absolutely knew this as I had seen it in countless movies. A shimmering lake of still blue water which, despite the burning sun, was crisp and cool as we swam in ecstasy together with our messianic leader... life would never again be the same.

Bernie, by the way, has no recollection of this event.

O, CANADA

(National Anthem of Canada)

One day in February, 1969, my parents mentioned that a cousin from Canada, whom we had never met, was arriving from South Africa to stay for a short while. I decided to spend that weekend at home in Westcliff in order to meet her, particularly as she was a female cousin.

Apparently, she had just spent six months visiting our mutual relatives in South Africa, and was on her way back to Canada via the UK.

Maple Karen Lee was the third child of my father's sister, Mary Gersholowitz, who had married and emigrated to Canada after the war. John, her father was not Jewish which had caused some difficulties for her mother's traditional Jewish family.

John was a very handsome man who looked like Clark Gable, and no doubt this must have attracted Mary. To the wider family he had a somewhat hazy background, having originally been born in Aldershot, and then lived as a child for some time in Devon. His latter childhood was spent in a small council house outside of Southampton with his foster mother, later known to us affectionately as 'Grandma Richards'.

John was extremely patriotic towards his adopted country, Canada, and named his new daughter and third child Maple Karen Lee as she was the only one born in Canada.

Since changing names seems to be an obsession in my family, in true family tradition we, in England called her by her second name, Karen. It just seemed easier.

Born in Oakville, she spent her youth in Crystal Beach a small lakeside resort within Fort Erie, Ontario, on the Niagara River and directly opposite Buffalo in New York State.

The Southend-on-Sea area had some similarities to Crystal Beach as it was, and still is, a seaside town attracting many day trippers to it's amusement parks and penny arcades.

Although her mother occasionally made chopped liver, Maple did not at all consider herself Jewish but according to Jewish law, of course, she was.

To me she had numerous attributes – she was beautiful, she was Jewish and she was very reserved, quiet even. I found this combination irresistible, especially the reserved part, which was a rarity in the girls that I knew.

At first, of course, I introduced her to my friends as my cousin, but very quickly it became apparent to everyone that we had developed a special bond that went well beyond being just cousins.

It is hard to describe how you feel when you meet your spiritual partner, how natural it is to be in their company.

Divine providence threw us together and from the moment that we met there really was no question that we would make our lives together.

She stayed in England, and the family started talking.

Years later, she told me that her mother used to joke about her marrying a nice Jewish boy with a red sports car but, at this point, her mother started to panic and immediately went to see a rabbi for the first time in about forty years, to check whether a marriage between first cousins was acceptable in the Jewish religion.

The rabbi confirmed that it was OK, even though I did not have a red sports car.

We all breathed a sigh of relief.

In the summer of 1970, Maple went to Canada to spend time with her mother who had, by then, become very ill. Sadly, it would be the last time she would see her mother alive.

Her mother died in September of that year but by then Mary knew that her daughter would soon return to the very bosom of her own family.

MAKE IT WITH YOU

(Bread)

Soon after meeting my cousin Maple Karen, I decided to leave my job in London, return to Southend and join the family business which had morphed into two dress shops, one in Southend and a new one in Chelmsford.

She was also working in the business and we became inseparable. The main shop, which was located just off the Southend High Street and traded under the name of 'Gladrags', became one of the most fashionable boutiques in the local area.

We were married in a civil marriage ceremony at Southend-on-Sea Registry Office on 24 March 1971.

For the local Jewish community, it was a strange choice because both of us were Jewish (according to Jewish law), and therefore the more obvious choice would have been the local synagogue.

However, for those who knew us well, they understood that Maple Karen, whose father was not Jewish, had effectively been brought up as an Anglican and therefore, from her perspective at least, a traditional Jewish wedding in a synagogue was a pretty bizarre option.

I, on the other hand, who at that time was by no means a religious person, did nevertheless have a pretty strong Jewish identity, so a church wedding was really not on the cards.

Little did we know that just two years hence we would be married according to the Laws of Moses and

Israel, and this time it would be in the Holy City of Jerusalem.

And so it was that, on that bright spring morning, a crowd of around forty close friends and family gathered at the Southend Civic Centre to witness the civil marriage of Derek Leonard Lewis, to Maple Karen Lee Hayes-Richards.

My parents hosted a party at their flat which, like all good Jewish receptions, included the usual delicacies and a good time was had by all including my maternal grandmother (Booba) who, whilst criticizing the nature of the marriage, could not stop eating the salt beef.

This was by no means the end of the festivities as we had organized a wedding party at the Gore Hotel in Kensington for our close friends.

The Gore Hotel, at that time, had a themed dining room called the 'Elizabethan Room' where the floor was covered with straw, minstrels played lyres and well endowed wenches served honey mead to the diners. We had, of course, reserved the large 'King and Queen' table in the centre of the room for our party.

I am not sure that the hotel could have anticipated such an enthusiastic response when, at the end of the meal, they offered everyone a clay pipe. The room soon filled with the sweet smell of Red Lebanese cannabis and Moroccan Keef.

The visiting American tourists, who had just chanced upon this uproarious occasion, clapped and cheered.

Southend Registry Office - 24th March 1971.

Bridge Over Troubled Waters

(Simon & Garfunkel)

It was fortunate that we had such a strong relationship because, shortly after we were married, certain aspects of our life went rapidly downhill. Karen's mother, who had been very ill, had died the previous September but now my dear mother, Lily, died suddenly at the age of 58 in the June of 1971. I was, shell shocked and my father was devastated.

Apart from the emotional trauma, my mother had also been a mainstay of our fashion business and within a couple of months the company had gone into a downward business spiral and collapsed.

Karen and I found ourselves unemployed and musing on how quickly things can change. We decided to take a break and accepted the offer of a belated honeymoon sponsored by my father-in-law in Canada.

In those days, the only way you could fly transatlantic cheaply was by being a member of a group charter organization and so we immediately joined the British Overseas Families Association and went to stay in Maple's bedroom in Jellicoe Crescent, London, Ontario.

After this brief respite we came back to England to, well, not very much.

However, David (my best friend Bernie's brother) had been working on a new business idea and was waiting for us to return, as it appeared that we two, were necessary for it's success.

It partly involved my old flat in Chelsea, which I had sublet to him previously, and, footwear. The former was to become the headquarters of the 'Sneaky Freakers' organization. The latter were 'trainers'.

In those days, and nowadays, it is hard to believe there were no trainers as we know them today, there were only 'plimsolls'. Plimsolls were available either in white (tennis) or black (school) but not in any colour. The sole (if you will excuse the pun) concession to colour, was the green trim on Dunlop Green Flash tennis shoes.

Within a couple of weeks we were living in my flat, in Kings Road, Chelsea, it was actually owned by an old client and which I rented. It was a small studio flat and became the formal address of the Sneaky Freakers company with a factory consisting of a garden shed in Hampstead.

We had a little white van and went to the shed each day. The shed was staffed by Karen, myself and half a dozen other hippies smoking marijuana. We were all painting psychedelic colours on white plimsolls to the sound of Crosby, Stills and Nash.

Amazingly, we began supplying the big London stores like Harrods and Escalade and became a small part of the *zeitgeist* of London in the early 1970s; Biba on Kensington Church Street, The Chelsea Drugstore, Mr Freedom and... Sneaky Freakers!

We worked out that what we really needed was about $100,000 in investment to buy some real production facilities in Korea, and then our business future would be secured and we would be well on the way to becoming hippie millionaires!

David went to New York to raise the money but I assume that he must have had had another agenda because he only purchased a one way ticket and we did not see him again until 1973!

All this was a bit of a disappointment, but it had been lots of fun and, always optimistic, we were looking for something new.

Our cousin David had been looking for someone to decorate his flat in the East End of London and so we decided to become jobbing decorators, as you do. For a small stipend and living accommodation we agreed to decorate his flat, during the course of which Karen burnished her reputation as the 'gloss queen' because of her patient painting of the woodwork.

Time to combine my property expertise with our renovation skills and find a deal!

We bought a small terraced house in Westcliff-on-Sea for £3,250, together with cousin Victor, as a project for conversion into two flats.

I arranged a mortgage of £3,150 and borrowed the £100 balance from Barclays Bank and Victor invested £800 for the conversion. Karen and I lived in the house while we organized its conversion and decoration and, after renting out the ground floor flat, we moved into the upper flat.

Ultimately, the project took a lot out of us physically and emotionally and we decided that living and working in Westcliff or Southend-on-Sea, did not have that much attraction any more, so, in what was the conclusion of my first property deal we sold our share of the house to cousin Victor.

This was achieved by transferring the mortage to him and he was more than happy to pay us £500 for our 50% share, as by that time the rental income covered the mortgage, and as his parents, who lived just around the corner, could look after the management of the property.

Our £500 stake, was just about enough to fund our next adventure and the plan was: give up everything and go somewhere, anywhere!

Friends of ours had gone to various exotic places. We considered India but the airfare sounded too expensive. A cheap hotel in Spain for the winter was another consideration, but after listening to a personal message from Crosby, Stills and Nash regarding the Marrakesh Express we thought that Morocco would be a more spiritually uplifting option.

MY SWEET LORD

(George Harrison)

During our first few months of marriage, it could be said that Karen and I struggled to find an identity as a married couple. My friends had become her friends and my relatives were already hers but where we fitted in within wider society was not clear. Were we to become a young couple living a middle class life in a provincial town 40 miles from London, or a hip and fashionable couple looking for a spiritual adventure?

We thought we would try the latter... at least for the time being.

So, in September of 1971, we decided to escape the English winter, and at the same time seek some spiritual truth by travelling overland to Morocco.

I bought a second hand Honda motorbike, which was the key to our first touring adventure as a married couple.

It was already getting cold as we headed down the A13 and at Dartford, after having travelled grand total of 26 miles, we faced the first challenge of our spiritual journey – where to find a local garage to fix a broken brake cable?

Undaunted we carried on. The ferry crossing from Dover to Calais was uneventful and we started off on our adventure of a lifetime.

After about 250 miles in the freezing cold and blinding rain of northern France, our faces were red raw, my Zapata moustache was iced up and the heels on Karen's fashionable boots were broken. Good start.

So, we loaded the bike into the baggage car of the train and headed 800 miles south to Biarritz. Some hours later, reunited with the bike, we crossed over to Spain at San Sebastian.

At last it was warm, as we passed through Burgos and Madrid, but somewhere on the road outside of Madrid, and approaching sunset, we suffered a puncture on the back wheel. The back wheel is obviously driven by the chain mechanism, and so that had to be removed completely before the puncture could be repaired.

A gentle old peasant farmer took us to his home which consisted of a courtyard, where he kept his donkey and cart and an upstairs room, where he kept his wife. By now it was dark and he brought out a rusty old oil lamp which he held over me as I fixed the bike.

I removed the wheel, patched up the puncture and replaced everything by which time my arms were covered in grease up to the elbows.

A quick application of Swarfega resolved the problem and my arms were clean. Our dear friend the farmer, who by virtue of his cart activities was well versed in the perils of grease, thought I had performed a miracle having never seen the wonder of Swarfega before.

In gratitude, I left him the jar so that he could perform his own miracles.

We stayed the night at a small hotel in Valdepeñas on the way to the Costa del Sol, and after café con leche on the terrace the next morning, we were again on the road. More trials, however, were to come.

The bike, which was apparently suffering from increasing levels of stress, stopped working just outside Granada.

It was not much fun waiting by the roadside in the heat of the Sierra Nevada, so we were very grateful when a jeep full of intoxicated Australians came down the road. They casually lifted the bike, myself and Karen into the jeep and took us to a repair shop in Malaga and after we got going again we made it to Algeciras.

"Are you Jewish?" Jacques asked on the ferry from Algeciras to Ceuta. This was not a question I expected to be asked by the first Moroccan I met. He seemed respectable, well dressed with fashionable aviator spectacles.

"Yes," I admitted, slightly bemused.

"Great," he said, "I am also Jewish and when you get to Casablanca you must come to visit my family."

By the time the ferry arrived in Ceuta, the Spanish enclave on the North African coast, we had become firm friends with Jacques and his friend Bebe and had given them our heavy rucksack to take to Casablanca, so that we could travel light. Jacques and Bebe drove off in their Fiat 127. We had yet to cross the border from Ceuta to Morocco.

The morose and unshaven guard at the border was somewhat menacing and insisted on my removing my motorbike helmet. When he saw the length of my hair, he refused us entry with a dismissive waive of the hand under the Kingdom's apparent 'no more hippies' regulations.

Some travellers who we had befriended suggested swimming around the bay to avoid the border guards, but after a little thought we came up with a simpler solution which did not take as much physical effort as swimming around the guards, and also had the advantage of being less dangerous.

Karen was trained as a hairdresser and as I was prepared to forego any hippie principles that I may have had about long hair, she cut off my hair and we were allowed in.

We took the scenic route through the dope growing region of Tetouan, towards the town of Fez and somewhat true to form I pushed on relentlessly until the sun had almost set. Of course we found ourselves on the open road, with no building in sight and no idea of where we could stay that night.

Somewhat desperately I asked some local shepherd boys, in broken French, if they knew of any place to stay. "*Il y a un hotel?*"

"*Non…*" they indicated that we should go with them and they led us, pushing the bike, to a single storey house which comprised two rooms and a compound for various animals. The boys' father and mother greeted us as honoured guests, and after a tagine of lamb and couscous the couple promptly vacated their bedroom and, with classic Arab hospitality, insisted that we slept in their bed for that night whilst they bunked in with their five kids in the other room.

In the morning, awaking to the beautiful smell of baghrir and coffee, we ate with them and bid farewell to this wonderful and humble family.

The next night we stayed at a pension in Meknes and in the morning headed for the coast, arriving in Casablanca towards the evening on the Friday of that week.

It was not difficult to find Jacque's house and we knocked on the door, which was answered by his father who excitedly welcomed us to his house. We were joined by his wife, Jacques and Jacque's sister, and ushered into the dining room where he was just about to say the Hebrew blessing over wine. It was, of course, the beginning of the Jewish Sabbath.

Jacque's father Monsieur Dayan, turned out to be a furniture maker to King Hassan. The King liked and respected the Jews over which he ruled, even though the general population were not unhappy to see 300,000 of them leave when the State of Israel had been formed 25 years earlier.

M Dayan insisted that we take the keys of an apartment which he had over one of his shops downtown and we stayed in the apartment for a few days, while we acclimatized.

On the first night I was sent on an errand by Karen to score some marijuana, which surprisingly was no mean feat. Of course we had unwittingly sailed through the dope growing district of Morocco and it would probably have been easy there, had we thought of it.

Casablanca, on the other hand, was a city and especially dark and foreboding after hours.

Anyway, I headed off to do my duty and after wandering around for quite a while found myself in the port area and went into a bar.

Just a bit of advice for any travellers who find themselves at night in the main town of a Muslim country which technically bans alcohol, and has a bad reputation… try not to end up in a bar down by the port!

I escaped the Norwegian sailor who propositioned me in the toilet of the bar, and quickly contributing lots of dirham for my share of wine, lest he and his friends accuse me of ripping them off, I left, fast.

After ten minutes I slowed down and found myself in one of those fabulous French boulevards in the centre of town, at which point a large African man stepped out of the shadows, and asked me if I wanted 'keef'. With palpitating heart the deal was done. On reflection, I think that Brixton would have been less intimidating.

Back at the apartment, Karen had made up sardine sandwiches and we spent the evening eating smoking and playing rummy, with the pack of cards we had brought along for the occasion. This was cool.

A few days later, according to plan, we went to a market in Rabat with Jacques and Bebe and sold the motorbike. We were now ready to board the Marrakesh Express.

Marrakesh Express

(Crosby, Stills and Nash)

The Marrakesh Express, immortalized by the song, refers to the iconic train which runs on the Moroccan rail network from Casablanca to Marrakesh, The system is part of the original French colonial railway built at the early part of the 20th century to transport goods and military personnel.

Graham Nash, who wrote the song, boarded the train, as we did from Casablanca and the trip took close to four hours. The atmosphere of third class is described in those famous lyrics,

"Looking at the world through the sunset in your eyes
Travelling the train through clear Moroccan skies
Ducks and pigs and chickens call
Animal carpet wall to wall
American ladies five foot tall in blue

Sweeping cobwebs from the edges of my mind,
Had to get away to see what we could find
Hope the days that lie ahead
Bring us back to where they've led
Listen not to what's been said to you..."

A few miles outside of Marrakesh, the train entered a long curve in the track, slowing to a crawl. In the distance numerous figures could be seen desperately running towards the train. Could it be that we were under attack? Not so unlikely in those days as there had been an attack on the palace, a mini revolution, the previous July.

As the *djelabba* clad men neared it could be seen that they were carrying kettles and pots. They all clambered aboard as the train slowed and proceeded to serve hot tea and boiled eggs to the passengers, which was very welcome after around three hours of travelling. Not so much a revolution but a Moroccan version of the restaurant car.

In my view, approaching Marrakesh on the train as the sun drops to the horizon is one of the great travel moments, with dusty pink houses set off against the lush green the palm trees. To this day, dusty pink and green is my favourite colour combination.

We settled in to a small Riad hotel, set around an orange tree, which housed a number of hippie travellers. Our host, Muhammad, slept across the front door at nights for added security.

A typical day consisted of a foray to the souk to eat lunch, usually omelette in French bread, and then watch the evening transformation of Jemaa el-Fnaa square into a vast tented food city. Back at the hotel we would join our new found friends, cook dinner on our tagines, and smoke keef.

Bob and Cheryl were an item, he, Canadian and she, American. They had been traveling the world together and had met up with Roger in Europe before arriving in Marrakesh. Bob was a wizened hippy with freckles and a goatee moustache, who collected goulimine beads and Cheryl was an all American blonde from Seattle.

Cheryl and Bob had originally planned to settle down on the 22 acres of wooded farmland which Bob owned in Lumby, just outside of Vancouver. That is, until Cheryl met Roger.

Roger, who towered over all of us at well over six foot, was a tall handsome cowboy type from Oregon, and to complicate all their lives Cheryl had fallen in love with him while they were in Europe. By the time we all met up in Marrakesh, they had arrived at an understanding which was that Cheryl would stay with Bob while they finished their travels, and then she would head off into the sunset with Roger.

It was by now the end of 1971 and we had been persuaded by our new found friends to spend Christmas in Marrakesh. The plan was that, in January, they would come back to the UK with us and go on from there to the US and Canada, and that is indeed what happened, although on the way we had to stop off at Barclay's Bank in Gibraltar so that I could somehow obtain enough money for our airfares.

For the first few weeks we all stayed back in the flat at Burdett Avenue, Westcliff-on-Sea, that is to say, at the house which was my first property deal. I rented the flat from Victor, bought a pinstripe three piece suit and secured a managerial job with Gross Fine & Kreiger Chalfen, a commercial estate agency in Mayfair.

During the 'sneaky freakers' period, when we were distributing our hand painted sneakers to various fashionable outlets and stores, the headquarters of our mini empire was an apartment in Chelsea. This apartment was owned by a previous client of mine and had been occupied by various friends during the periods Karen and I were away, but now I reclaimed my rightful heritage, a tiny studio flat at a modest rental of £5 per week.

The guys went home, Bob to Vancouver... and Cheryl with Roger to Oregon. I started work in London, and ensconced on the Kings Road, Karen and I spent the next two years in swinging Chelsea...

I Can See Clearly Now

(Johnny Nash)

To say that life had been a bit of a roller coaster for the first year of our marriage is a bit of an understatement, but, after we returned from our Moroccan adventure we moved back into the London flat with a view to leading a more conventional lifestyle. Maybe it was not quite so conventional but the next couple of years were good and various clouds had dissipated.

It was a tiny studio flat on the second floor of 541a Kings Road, SW6. The building had a shop on the ground floor and another flat on the first floor and was owned by Ted Kleinman, who had been a client of mine before I had met Karen when I worked for Henry Berney.

Originally, the previous tenant had done a bunk and left the flat in a terrible state. Ted had instructed me to take possession and when, at the time, I had offered to take over the tenancy at £5 a week he happily agreed. The rent was cheap even in those days and I had lived there briefly, cleaned up the place and then sublet the flat to various friends. Now I had taken it back permanently.

At that time the locality, called World's End, was known as a poor area but a pretty cool and trendy place to live, being opposite Chelsea Football Club's home ground at Stamford Bridge and at the western end of London's most fashionable shopping street.

I had started a new job as manager of the West End Offices department at Gross Fine and Krieger Chalfen.

Karen became a housewife and we settled down into what was to become our first real marital home. Two guys worked in my department, Ian and Robert, and they became good friends. They would often come over for Karen's famous spaghetti bolognaise. I am still in touch with them.

The flat originally consisted of a large studio room, kitchen and bathroom but with some deft DIY, I managed to convert the kitchen into a bedroom, and relocate the sink, oven and fridge into the tiny entrance hall.

In the bedroom I built a platform bed with a foam mattress, which was about three foot off the floor to give us storage room underneath. Also there was a set of steps for the dog.

Oh, sorry did I not tell you about the dog? Yes, well there was plenty of room, so we decided to get a dog, from Battersea Dogs Home. She was a black mongrel and we named her Biba, after the famous fashion store in London. Our friend Belle Rubin (Bernie's sister) was once a dog walker for the famous Barbara Hulanicki's Doberman Pincers, she being the owner of Biba... but I digress.

Biba, the dog, not the store, settled in and had a lovely temperament, unlike our only other experience with a dog which was cousin Ian's pure bred Afgan Hound which he had dumped on us when he was off to warmer climes.

We had fun in that flat, which was decorated with a beautiful Indian carpet and huge cushions and, well... not much else, but friends came, Karen cooked and we went to new restaurants and generally enjoyed ourselves. Karen became part of the local scene, helped out in the local charity shop and sponsoring an adventure playground for local kids. I learned a lot from Karen about how to treat average people, because she had no hang-ups about class and mixed quite easily with those that would be considered by the middle classes in England to be 'hoi polloi'.

At one point during 1971, a business acquaintance of mine who had left the property field, acquired the shop downstairs and converted it to a restaurant which he called 'Tweedledum'. The grand opening, to which we were duly invited, was a memorable occasion, not least because of the presence of Christine Keeler who, of course, was one of the call girls and main protagonists in the Profumo Affair, which had taken place only a few years earlier.

However, the really memorable part of the evening came as people realised that someone had spiked the punch with LSD. We were lucky because we just had to crawl upstairs but how others got home, I will never know.

Karen's sister Jackie had been at our wedding in early 1971, and came the next year with her husband, Alfred. They came for just one week.

We thought it would be nice to take them to Paris to give them a taste of exotic Europe. In those days there was no Eurostar, and we did not at that time have a car. So we hired one and set off early one morning, caught the ferry from Dover and drove to Paris. We saw the sights, went up the Eiffel Tower and stayed overnight in a small hotel that we knew on the Rue de Sommerard. The next day we had lunch and drove back. It was a good effort and a great trip.

Later in that week, we met up with a crowd of our friends at the famous Halepi Restaurant in Bayswater (it is still there). We had smoked some weed before going, and a riotous dinner followed with flowing wine. Some of us went outside for a breath of fresh air and one of us... collapsed.

We were worried, but the ambulance men less so. It was the first time that anyone had seen the 'drunk tank' at the local hospital. For two conservative teachers from Northern Ontario that is a week they will not forget.

Towards the end of 1972, TWA (Trans World Airlines) were offering a special deal for passengers flying out of the UK. If passengers made a minimum of three stops in the USA, then the flight was half-price!

Why would this interest us? Well, the town where Karen's sister lived, Sault Ste Marie, Ontario is a twin city with Sault Ste Marie, Michigan and on the American side was an airport. I worked out that we could fly to New York, stay overnight with cousin Andrew (brother of the owner of the Afgan Hound), fly to Detroit the next day, and then fly up to Sault Ste Marie, Michigan. Hey presto, three stops and we would be there for Christmas.

Well, it worked, but the size of the planes can be best described by the food served on them. The first leg was a great breakfast and then a wonderful airline dinner on a 747, the second was a nice lunch on a 737 and the third was a boiled sweet on the 'Hopper' stopping at Flint, Travers City and Sault Ste Marie.

The airport on the US side was really quite small but fully staffed including one man to clear the runway, the same man to guide the plane in, and guess what, the same man to unload the baggage!

At least our family picked us up. They had a great time as they had never before been to the airport at Sault Ste Marie, Michigan, even though it was only 25 miles from their house.

SAULTE STE MARIE

(Dean Martin)

Karen (Maple) and I sat attentively in a pew which was not too close to the pulpit, not too far from the exit. It was Christmas Day 1972 in Saulte Ste Marie and the low slung Baptist Church, gleamed in the pristine snow, crisp and clean as a picture postcard.

"Just as Jesus came down from the Mount, so I will come down from the pulpit into the congregation," intoned the preacher. Uh oh, I thought, I am sure he is looking at me. Then I remembered, no problem, I'm related to half the congregation.

I had married Karen at Southend Registry Office a year earlier and we were visiting her sister. Jackie had married into a respected Baptist family in Sault Ste Marie, a steel town in North Ontario (which confusingly has a French name, but a large Italian community). Anyway, I was well connected and we were honoured guests.

Apparently it was the custom to convey Christmas greetings from far flung areas and the preacher would announce these in a loud voice... 'and we have Christmas greetings from... (so and so)... in Timmins/ Kalamazoo/Sudbury.' He kept looking over at me, and slowly it dawned on me that he wanted to announce greetings from London, England.

Notwithstanding that my complexion was a little on the swarthy side, London, England was such an impressive place to people living 500 miles north of civilization so I decided that he would even accept Christmas greet-ings from me. I gave him the nod...

The service ended with us standing outside the Church, together with the preacher, as each member of the congregation, who now felt that they knew us personally, came up to shake our hands.

We did not know at this point that a year later we would emigrate to Israel to begin a new phase of our lives, seeking the truth, as religious Jews... no more Christmases for us.

I'M WILLIN'

(Seatrain)

In truth, David Rubin was not, initially anyway, my friend, rather he was my best friend's brother, which obviously accorded him a certain status but he was a couple of years older than me, and somewhat strange and solitary in the early years.

I shared a large part of my teenage years with Bernie Rubin, and his dear sister Belle and we have a bond to this day, even though Bernie now lives in Australia and Belle, lives in Israel.

Having said that, David had a significant influence on my life and this now extended to Karen and myself as a married couple. Whether that is to his merit or he was just a tool of divine providence, I will let you judge.

Our early careers had followed a somewhat similar path in that he had become a commercial property agent in London and we would often meet up in the West End plotting how we were going to make our fortunes.

David however was very much an adventurer and the boring life of an agent was not for him. He was a more lateral thinker, and I admired that part of his personality.

After he gave up the property business he travelled extensively, which included going on the hippy trail to India, coming back overland through Afghanistan and Jordan. In 1967 he was one of the last travellers to pass through the famed Mandlebaum Gate into Israel, just before the start of the Six-Day War.

He had subsequently travelled back and forth to Israel and finally settled there.

And so, when he arrived at our flat in the Kings Road wearing an embroidered Yemenite *yarmulke* on his head, we listened to him with fascination as he described the yeshiva (Jewish religious college) in Jerusalem where he was studying, and which, according to him, was definitely the place to find spiritual redemption.

After the Six-Day War, the charismatic Rabbi who was dean of the yeshiva had gathered together a number of Jewish boys and girls from America and England and had begun teaching them religious texts, but primarily the Babylonian Talmud which previously had not been taught in English, at least not to those people without a religious background, and therefore had been relatively inaccessible to those not expert in Aramaic, Hebrew or Yiddish.

These texts showed that the Jews had a rich spiritual heritage and that it really was not necessary for Jews to go to India or seek gurus to achieve spiritual understanding; we had it all in our own writings and historical texts.

The pitch was very persuasive and within a few weeks, we were working out how we could, once again, extricate ourselves from the humdrum life we had made for ourselves.

After all, we were at the prime of our lives, we had travelled, we had smoked dope, indeed we had experimented with psychedelic drugs, as did Aldous Huxley when he wrote *Brave New World* and Francis Crick when he discovered the double helix structure of DNA.

Now we needed spiritual sustenance to move forward to greater heights and if that meant becoming religious Jews, then we were up for it.

MORNING HAS BROKEN

(Cat Stevens)

Two years had now passed since we had returned from Morocco and, in July of 1973, I resigned my position as the manager of West End offices at Gross, Fine & Krieger Chalfen.

We had scraped together what money we could, packed a large school trunk with our meagre possessions, including a small lightweight tent. We booked two one way tickets on El Al airlines, to the newly named Ben Gurion Airport, together with a reservation for a tranquillized dog in the hold. We were not going anywhere, without Biba.

You may express surprise that we were taking a tent, but we did not have a lot of money and we thought it would be a good idea to have a modest camping holiday for a couple of weeks before we began our holy studies. Also, even though David had assured us that accommodation was not a problem, I wanted to cover all eventualities.

Karen had never slept under canvas before and the last time I had been in a tent was on a school camping trip to the low countries when I had been 14 years old.

So, our last night in England was spent testing out the tent, duly pitched in the back garden of Bernie's shoe shop in Benfleet.

JERUSALEM OF GOLD

(Ofra Haza)

To appreciate the next part of my story the reader will need a little more Near East history and geography.

Although the Jews had been expelled from the Old City of Jerusalem in 1948, they had, at the cost of many lives, retained the modern western part of the city (outside the walls of the Old City) together with a land corridor to the Mediterranean coast.

Nineteen years later, in 1967, Israel had been threatened with extinction by its Arab neighbours and Israel's overall military strategy was first, to try to deal with Egypt in the south, then with Syria to the north but they were deeply worried about an attack from Jordan. A secret message was sent to King Hussein to the effect that as long as he did not attack Israel from the east, then Israel would not attack Jordan.

King Hussein of Jordan was an honourable and respected military man who had been educated at Harrow and Sandhurst Military School, and knew that the Israelis were as good as their word, but ultimately he could not resist the political pressure from Gamal Abdel Nasser of Egypt and the other Arab States to strike at Israel, and so he did.

During the ensuing action, later acknowledged as one of the greatest military victories of modern warfare, Israel conquered the Sinai Desert, the Golan Heights and the West Bank of the River previously held by the Hashemite Kingdom of Jordan. The real prize, however was the Old City of Jerusalem which Israel annexed and re-unified.

In the action to secure the Old City, some of the worst fighting took place around Zion Gate. Just outside this gate to the South West is the area known as Mount Zion, which overlooks the Dome of the Rock and the Al Aksa Mosque, otherwise known as the Temple Mount, and also overlooks the Mount of Olives.

Prior to the 1967 reunification of Jerusalem the ceasefire line of 1948 (known as the 'Green Line') had run through Mount Zion so that to the East was a strip of no man's land, the Eastern part of the city being, at that time, controlled by Jordan.

Access to Mount Zion before 1967 was from the new part of the city but, dedicated pilgrims who wanted to get to King David's Tomb could only do so by climbing a series of steps from where the Hebron Road met the valley to the West of the mountain, enabling them to gain access to the roof above the Tomb.

There they would pray while being careful not to expose themselves to Jordanian snipers, who would shoot at them from the other side of the no man's land.

Later, during the time I was working as his assistant, Rabbi Dr S. Z. Kahane would tell me the story of how he, as Director General of Israel's Ministry of Religious Affairs, came to control the mountain:

"After fierce fighting the army finally broke through Zion Gate and I was called to Mount Zion by Moshe Dayan, who was, at that time, the Minister of Defence. He was standing in the courtyard opposite the entrance to King David's Tomb which looks out over the Mount of Olives and he said, 'Shin Zayin (my name), as you are the Director General of the Ministry of Religious

*Affairs, and this is a holy site, I now hand Mount Zion
and the Tomb of King David to you to look after and
supervise.'*

*I said to him, 'Moshe, under the circumstances, you
will need to give this to me in writing,' whereupon he
took a piece of paper and a pen, and confirmed the
administrative transfer to me, there and then."*

Dr Kahane, with me at his side (I had become his
assistant), would later confirm this story to the five
judges of the Supreme Court of Israel during the legal
case of 'Israel Lands Authority v The Mount Zion
Committee'. He proudly showed them the paper given
to him by Moshe Dayan.

Rabbi Dr S. Z. Kahane was a member of the
Mizrachi political party and considered himself somewhat of a spiritual visionary. He was the author of a
quasi mystical book called the *Legends of Zion* and was
dedicated to the Biblical principle of the 'ingathering
of the exiles'; the core idea of the Religious Zionist
movement.

He was determined to influence the ingathering in a
practical and real way, by retaining his chairmanship of
the Mount Zion Committee even after his retirement
from the Ministry of Religious Affairs. In this way he
would be able to implement his plan.

From 1967 onwards, he effectively controlled Mount
Zion himself and therefore he had a prime, though hotly
disputed, piece of real estate in Jerusalem where he
planned to establish a religious school to bring young
secular Jews back to their religion and their spiritual heritage. At that time many Western educated Jewish kids
were visiting Israel in the wake of the Six-Day War, and
so he had a pool of potential students to draw from.

All he needed was a charismatic teacher, a *Rosh HaYeshiva* (Head of the College) to motivate young Jewish kids to learn about their heritage and study the Torah... in English, because most of the youngsters coming to Israel were English speakers.

The concept of teaching serious Torah subjects in English to previously secular kids was, at that time, quite revolutionary. Until then, only youngsters from ultra orthodox Jewish communities had the background to access the necessary texts, specifically the Talmud which is written in Aramaic.

More significantly the language of instruction in most established *Yeshivot* (colleges) had been either Hebrew or more often Yiddish, the high German language of the Jews who lived in Eastern Europe.

Rabbi Mordechai Goldstein was originally from the Bronx in New York and although his parents were middle-of-the-road orthodox Jews, they had sent him to the famous *Yeshiva Chofetz Chaim* in Queens, where he studied under the tutelage of Rabbi Henoch Leibowitz.

He stayed there for 18 years until finally Rabbi Leibowitz sent him 'out into the world', and he arrived in Israel with his wife in 1967.

And so, as they say, to cut a long story short, *Yeshiva Hatfutsot* the *Diaspora Yeshiva* was established on Mount Zion in 1967, with Rabbi Goldstein as Dean and Rabbi Dr S. Z. Kahane as President, to facilitate the 'ingathering of the exiles' and begin the messianic process. The first recruits were some of the erstwhile college students from America and the UK who flocked to Jerusalem in the wake of the Six-Day War and could be found hanging around the Western (wailing) Wall and other high profile tourist locations. They were duly housed in the crumbling Crusader ruins that surrounded King David's Tomb and introduced to the esoteric teaching of their forefathers.

It is to this place, in 1973 (or 5733 in the Hebrew Calendar), that Karen and I would head to seek spiritual truth and redemption.

'MI ADIR'

(A Jewish wedding song)

Upon arrival we headed to Netanya on the coast of Israel, and checked into a campsite.

I felt that we needed some general acclimatization before we went up to Jerusalem to begin our spiritual journey. We chose Netanya because I knew the Wilson family who had made *Aliyah* (emigrated to Israel) in the early sixties. Mary was the sister of my auntie Ray and was a tour guide, and her husband, Morry worked in the dry cleaning section of the Dan hotel in Tel Aviv. I had been in contact with them when I had been in Israel in 1967.

The owner of the campsite was a gruff *chalutznik* (pioneer) who, when we told him of our mission, shook his head and looked at us as if we were quite mad. His advice was to have a nice holiday and then go home.

This man represented one sector of the population in Israel, the pioneers, whose families came over from Eastern Europe before the second world war, with a secular ideology influenced by communism. They cleared the swamps, built the land with their bare hands and fought for the independence of the State.

I had certainly identified with them when I had come in 1967, but now we had come to study and try to understand those on the other side of the ideological spectrum. The religious one.

Meanwhile, we were faced with our first problem. It turned out that there really were no facilities for married couples within the yeshiva campus, to say nothing of the fact that, since we had not had a religious wedding we were not even married according to Jewish law!

Minor details that David Rubin had not mentioned.

We had two options. We could temporarily split up, with me living in the yeshiva and Karen living in the girls' dormitory in the Jewish Quarter or alternatively we could get an apartment in town, live as a couple and in due course get married, again! We chose the latter.

David had spoken with a friend, Asher Levy, who owned a furniture store downtown and his mother had a place to rent next to her apartment in Geula. Geula is an area surrounding a famous street in Jerusalem called Mea Shearim (the Street of a Hundred Gates).

To set the scene then, this area known as Geula is located outside the walls of the Old City of Jerusalem and looks like (and to all intents and purposes, is) an early 19th century Russian or Polish village. Almost all of the inhabitants are ultra-orthodox Jews, the men dressed in long black coats and wide brimmed hats, sporting *payot* (earlocks), and the women scuttle along in drab shapeless dresses wearing headscarfs or ill fitting wigs. There are posters on the walls warning any tourists that immodest dress will not be tolerated.

Gveret (Mrs) Levy was one of a few Persian Jews who lived in the area and, because of her oriental background was, when compared to a Polish Hassid, a relatively tolerant person. She did not have any objection to our little black dog, the sight of which, for each of the other inhabitants of the area, was roughly the equivalent of a red rag to a bull. The dog was considered 'impure' and therefore fair game for the children who were quick to throw stones at the dog and sometimes, at us.

Adjoining her apartment, she had a rickety lean-to extension consisting of two rooms; kitchen and bathroom. Modest was an understatement.

Nevertheless, we settled in as best we could and went to the yeshiva campus each day to study. In separate classrooms of course.

Apart from the yeshiva of which he was president, Rabbi Dr S. Z. Kahane, as chairman of the Mount Zion Committee, had given various people rights to occupy certain areas of Mount Zion over the years.

One of these was Rabbi Nyman, who lived with his wife in an apartment which formed part of the buildings surrounding King David's Tomb.

The thing about Rabbi Nyman was that he was never without his *Tanach* (Bible) and he had a photographic memory for biblical names.

Karen had not been given a Hebrew name at birth and she wanted and indeed needed a formal biblical name, so we duly went to see Rabbi Nyman.

He flicked through the Tanach and stopped at the Book of Job, where he showed us that one of the daughters of Job was called *Keren HaPuch*, and accordingly she adopted the shortened version 'Keren'.

For those readers with an understanding of Hebrew, *Keren HaPuch* means an 'upside down horn' and refers to the vessel in which women kept their cosmetics during biblical times.

Keren is now quite a common name in Israel but, in 1973, the use of it was considered very innovative.

So, within a few weeks of arriving in Israel we were dressed in full religious garb, living in the most religious part of town and observing all the necessary rituals.

We needed to get married.

The *Rosh HaYeshiva* (Head Rabbi of the yeshiva) was away for the summer but the Chief Rabbinate of Jerusalem introduced us to an English speaking Rabbi.

Rabbi Alexander Carlebach, who had formerly been the Chief Rabbi of Belfast, had recently retired to Jerusalem and he agreed to supervise our wedding on Mount Zion, so we chose a date.

Tu B'Av is a very propitious day in the Hebrew calendar. A Talmudic story recounts how this was a semi-festival, and in those days young girls would go out to the fields dressed in white to find themselves husbands. We decided to get married on that day.

We both started a 'nil by mouth' fast 25 hours before the wedding. At midnight, the night before, I was taken for immersion in a secret ritual bath located in the adjoining Arab village of Silwan and reputedly used by the High Priest in the times of the Temple. The next day Karen visited Zufnicks, the ritual baths in Geula,

And so, under the full moon of the 15th day of the Hebrew month of Menachem Av 5733, Karen walked around me seven times, I spoke the words, *'ha're, ut m'kudeshet li...'* (behold you are holy to me...) and we were married with *chupah and kiddushin* (canopy and holy blessing) on Mount Zion overlooking the Mount of Olives and close to the site of the Holy Temple. According to the Gregorian calendar the date was 13 August 1973.

GRAVITY

(John Mayer)

During the course of writing this book, I found that it helped the process to think about such mundane matters as which font to use, how to title each chapter and generally how to present the text on the page. When I mentioned this to my children *en passant*, they were amused at the idea that I had approached it in this manner, rather than concentrating on the content.

I explained to them that, since I had always been a bit of a story teller, in truth, the actually content was not so much the problem because somehow there always seemed to be stuff to verbalise, the question was how to put pen to paper and I found that the easiest way was to make the frame and then, so to speak, insert the painting.

I had learned from various esoteric studies that form as well as force is needed to move to greater spiritual heights.

At this point I would also like to say that while I had started to write in chronological order, I do not feel constrained to continue in that vein. Moreover, as I now begin to describe how Karen and I moved on to the more spiritual aspects of our life, it occurs to me that a little religious philosophy is called for and what better way than to start with The Creation?

Here is an comparatively recent email exchange of mine, about the subject of Creation.

"Dear Professor,

Thank you for your letter and it is indeed I, who commented on your letter. What a pity we could not continue the jousting in the full glare of the JC readership!

Unfortunately, I do not have a copy of the original article or your letter but I think I recall the general thrust of both the former and the latter.

I agree that in the case of apparent contradictions we may on occasion need to re-think how the Torah is interpreted and, provided that such interpretation does not undermine certain fundamental principles of the Torah, I do not have a problem with that concept.

On the contrary, if I recall correctly, one of the very points I was making was that in regard to the Torah generally and Genesis in particular, such interpretations already exist and the problem was that in your letter you were not comparing 'like with like' but you were juxtaposing apparently sophisticated scientific 'fact' with religious thought which you seemed to be characterising as primitive and indeed ridiculous.

This, of course, is a well rehearsed argument along the lines of 'how can you possibly say that the world was created in seven days when fossil evidence is found which is 40,000 years old, or indeed when our scientists tell us that the universe is 14 billion years old ...?'

One of the midrashic reasons given for why the Garden of Eden is described as the Pardess (orchard) is because the four letters of the Hebrew word (i.e. PRDS) refer to Pshat (simple meaning), Remez (allusion), Drash (explanation) and Sod (secret), so there are different levels of meaning, but just because there is a profound meaning that does not, in itself, invalidate the simple meaning, because sometimes, we need the simple idea (for children, being one obvious example).

This can be compared to needing the Newtonian concept of gravity, which happens to suit our purposes (not least because it works). This, however, does not detract from the fact that Einstein proved that rather than objects being attracted by a fundamental force which acts between bodies the effects of that which we call 'gravity' are, as you say, a feature of the curvature of the space-time continuum.

So, in saying that Einstein proved that gravity 'does not exist', I admit I was somewhat playing with semantics, although you may be interested to note that the famous string theory physicist Eric Verlinde on the heels of Einstein does indeed subscribe to that position and said quite clearly 'for me gravity does not exist'.

Moving ahead to your comment about dismissing the science as a passing fad, I would not have put it that way myself but two memorable quotes do come to mind as supporting such a notion –

The first is from Bertrand Russell who famously said, 'Although this may seem a paradox, all exact science is dominated by the idea of approximation,' and the second from Arthur C. Clarke who more directly said, 'If an eminent professor states that something is undoubtedly true, then it is likely to be proved false the next day.'

Scientific theories of course confuse the public by parading themselves as provable in the same way as mathematical theories are provable, and this is just not true. Scientific theory is effectively based on a judicial system, i.e. proof beyond reasonable doubt, whereas for the most part mathematics relies on infallible logic...

Finally, with respect to your penultimate paragraph, I am not sure I remember the exact context, but I believe you were suggesting the story in Bereishit (Genesis) was implausible because the grass and vegetation were created on the third day but the sun was not created until the fourth day and therefore the plants would not have had any sunlight and therefore... how did they grow?

You say that you could not understand the point I was making by reference to 'artificial light'.

It is extraordinary, with respect, that you hold your hands out in amazement when you read a story about God making plants grow without the sun, because this, you maintain, is ridiculous, no sun, no photosynthesis... no plants... and, this seems to you a perfectly reasonable position to take?

But, and this is the point I was making, if you were to be told that plants could grow under artificial light, or hydroponically you would not, for one moment, challenge this as being ridiculous... this scenario would be totally believable and acceptable to you because it would be 'scientific'... even though there was no sun!

Do you see the inconsistency?

With kind regards..."

"Thank you for your email of 16 December and I have now found a copy of my original letter to the JC.

I am sorry if you felt my letter was aggressively critical, and the more so if you thought that I was dodging the question, of how one might interpret Bereishit to avoid... (the) mis-match with science.

This is clearly not a simple task, and if I knew all the answers, I would be the moshiach (the messiah)!

However, I thought in my letter that I would at least take a good stab at starting a conversation, by suggesting that the scientific theory of the age of the universe (c.14 billion years), could be accommodated by explaining that since, according to the account of creation, the sun was created on the 4th day, then at the very least the first three 'days' could not have been 24 hour days, because obviously in order to have a 24 hour day, you need the sun!

So the point was and indeed is, intended to demonstrate that even for someone who assumes that the creation is describing a simple time period of 7 x 24 hour days... this is not necessarily the case.

I know you are concerned as to whether views are widely held, so I will try to quote the Jewish sources, where I can.

There are famous commentaries on the meaning of the first word of the Torah, i.e. 'Bereishit', and the Rishonim (i.e. Rashi, Ibn Ezra etc. c.1,000 – 1,400 CE) all have a question... on the fact that the word Bereishit, in Hebrew grammar, is in the construct form, which broadly means that it is connected to another word, so they query the translation... 'In the beginning'... of what?

A number refer to earlier Rabbis (of the Mishna and Gemara 200–600 CE) who explain this by saying that 'reishit' refers to the Torah and the prefix 'Be...' instead of meaning 'in', in this instance, it is used actually as a preposition meaning 'for'.

Therefore the word Bereishit does not refer to a period of time at all, but actually means 'For the Torah'... in other words the heavens and the earth were created for that specific purpose, i.e. for the Torah.

Rashi then says, interestingly, that the waters were created before the heavens and the earth.

Now, we know that astronomers have compiled evidence that what we've always thought of as the actual universe – me, you, planets, stars, galaxies, all the matter in space – represents a mere 4% of what's actually out there.

The rest they call, for want of a better word, dark: 23% is something they call 'dark matter', and 73% is something even more mysterious, which they call 'dark energy'.

So, let's get this right, in the story of creation, at the very beginning of the Torah, in the very first words, we are told that within the context of an unmeasurable period of time the (earth) was 'unformed and void' and darkness was on the face of the deep'… that actually, sounds like a scientific description to me!

With reference to light, and to your question, 'Are you saying that creation also included the formation of some sort of artificial (non-sun) source of light and heat that bathed the earth for billions of years until the sun came on the scene?'

Well, first, the story of creation clearly says that 'light' as in… 'Let there be light', was created on 'day' one.

This was not 'artificial' light (why would God need something artificial?), but rather 'archetypal' as described by Rabbi Isaac Luria (1534–1572) known as the Ari… Before all things were created… the Supernal Light was simple and it filled all existence…

As I said above, the earth was not created first, but (if) being created before the sun then it would have been bathed in a Supernal light, but that would not necessarily have to have been for 'billions' of years, just actually for seven 'days' (however long that is?).

This, for me, is not critical for the growth of plants, but for the sake of the discussion, I am merely demonstrating to you that light existed prior to the sun, according to the account of creation.

I cannot sign off this letter without coming back to the question of gravity.

You accuse me of standing on record as claiming something that is totally untrue... (but) it really does depend on your definition of gravity, because if you explain it as an apple falling from the tree (i.e. Newton), then of course the statement is not correct, but, as I am sure you know, I was not using the word in that context.

I was always struck by the concept of the windowless rocket (author: I meant to say 'elevator') in space. According to Einstein's initial thought process the occupant's experience of the acceleration of the rocket (elevator) (i.e. having no reference points outside) was the same as if the occupant was experiencing gravity on earth.

Ultimately, Einstein arrived at the conclusion that the two experiences were not just similar, but were one and the same, in other words gravity was actually acceleration, (within the context of the space-time continuum).

Furthermore, with reference to Eric Verlinde, he did not just 'quip' the statement, 'for me gravity does not exist', it is very much at the heart of his work, which a quick Google search will establish.

Finally, please do not be surprised that I am willing to throw in my lot with a theoretical physicist, specialising in string theory because, believe it or not, I love *science and in fact, you may be interested to know that the latest string theories which postulate many parallel universes, were very much presaged by the Ramban (Nachmanides) in the thirteenth century!*

Kind regards…"

"…I think we would both agree that the subject of the creation of the world/universe is, one way or the other, a deeply profound one and I must say that it is a bit of a stretch to refer to your questions as 'simple'."

"Well, on reflection the questions may seem simple but the answers are not.

So, before answering, here is a short preamble, and then an explanation of each answer.

In interpreting the story of creation in light of current scientific thought (which is, after all, the object of the exercise) it is probably best to try to define the latter, first.

Therefore, for the sake of argument, let us say… for the time being (and I say for the time being because of course, scientific theories change), that I subscribe to something along the lines of the 'Big Bang' theory as an event which gave rise to our very own 'Space-Time Continuum' as envisaged by Albert Einstein.

Of course, the easiest reconciliation of the apparent anomaly of the first few verses of the creation story would be to say that the first three 'days' of the Bible were merely a general description of a process, which is repeated… (by way of explanation) in greater detail in the next three 'days'.

Alternatively, the creation of the sun and the moon on the fourth 'day', could have been, a description of, in effect, the Big Bang, giving rise to the Space-Time Continuum.

If that was the case, then according to that definition, prior to the fourth day of creation, 'time' itself may not have existed.

So, to your first question:

> 'Do you believe/accept that the earth was formed before the sun?'

Answer: No

If the first three days were a general description, followed by more detail then the answer is no, because the sun and the moon were created at the same time. (Which I think these days is supported by some if not most scientific 'theories' about the coagulation of galaxies, gas clouds etc.)

On the other hand, in the second scenario above, time may not have existed at all, prior to the fourth day, in which case I would take the position that the first three days would have been describing purely spiritual events because those type of events are not necessarily time-bound, and so my answer would also be no, because the earth would not have been physically formed before the sun, but rather it's apparent existence would have been in archetypal form, that is, as a manifestation in the mind of the Creator.

As regards the next question:

> 'Do you accept that the earth rotates around the sun and is held in place by that rotation?'

Answer: No, not necessarily.

I have referred to this in previous correspondence, but to reiterate, Einstein came to the conclusion around 1916 *(which is part of his special theory of relativity) that gravity and acceleration were essentially the same thing.*

He imagined a windowless elevator in space (i.e. a weightless environment) and postulated that if the floor was accelerating upwards at a given speed, a man inside would experience precisely the same effects as if he was standing on the ground. This enabled him to come to the revelatory conclusion that gravity was not, in fact, a force in the Newtonian sense of the word, but rather an effect of an accelerating motion of an object.

Therefore, the reason that the earth is rotating around the sun is not because it is held in place by that rotation (i.e. by a force) rather, the earth is accelerating along what would otherwise be a straight line, if it were not for the curvature of the space-time continuum, i.e. the fabric of space, which is in turn warped by the mass of the sun.

Finally to your last question:

> *'Is it your view that prior to the creation of the sun, the earth was bathed in some other form of light which also warmed the earth and created the earth's seasons and climates?'*

Answer: Yes and No.

Just to recap the story, a primeval and spiritual light was created on day one. The Creator separated the waters and formed the firmament of Heaven on the second day. On the third day (archetypal earth, seas are created) and archetypal plants are nourished by the primeval light. On the fourth day the original primeval light retreats to the firmament of Heaven and the sun and the moon take over the seasons and climates...

After creation, when the world was completed in its physical form it would continue to take instruction from the archetypal world. The Rabbis would later say in the Babylonian Talmud, 'not a blade of grass grows on earth, without it's equivalent in heaven striking it, and saying – 'grow!'

Regards..."

TRADITION

(Topol)

Living in Geula was an intense experience not least because we had jumped in at the deep end of religious life.

I grew a long beard, wore a black *yarmulke* (head covering) and *tzitzit* (a fringed garment) and Karen wore long modest dresses and covered her hair with a scarf.

Although we later actually lived on Mount Zion, at that time there were no residential facilities for married couples on the mountain so, in common with a number of couples, we lived in town. Together we constituted the married community of the Diaspora Yeshiva, known in the yeshiva world as the Kollel.

So, while we lived in our little apartment in Mea Shearim, most of the single guys lived in the old Crusader buildings built over King David's tomb and the single girls lived in shared apartments in the Jewish Quarter of the Old City, a short walk from the yeshiva..

Geula was also relatively close to Mount Zion and every day Karen and I would either walk, or get the No 1 bus, and on Friday nights we would have our Shabbat (Sabbath) dinner there.

The single guys and girls at the Diaspora Yeshiva were mostly college kids who had found their way to Jerusalem, searching for spirituality and truth.

Most of them were from America, many having been brought up as Reform Jews but there were a smaller number of kids from other countries including England, France and Israel. There were also a number of non- Jews who wanted to convert to Judaism.

In my case, it was not that difficult to learn the outer manifestations of the religion. In common with most Jewish kids of my generation in the UK, I had learned to read Hebrew as a youngster.

Although my parents were not religious, my maternal grandparents were traditional, and we had spent many a Friday night at their house having dinner.

I had celebrated my bar mitzvah at 13 years old and as a family we had invariably held or attended an annual Passover meal. I had been to Hebrew classes three times a week, and so the rituals and many of the biblical stories were familiar to me.

Karen, who had known nothing of Judaism until she left Canada, soaked up information like a sponge.

For both of us, after a short while, making blessings over food and drink, saying grace after meals and praying three times a day became second nature and around three months into our adventure we behaved and looked like a religious couple, slightly unconventional it has to be said, but seriously religious nevertheless.

Rituals leaned by rote, however, are not the difficult part of any religion. Understanding the philosophy and the morality of Judaism was the challenge.

By day I mostly studied the Babylonian Talmud while Karen spent time on other writings including the Prophets, the *Midrash* (Homiletic explanations) and the Code of Jewish Law.

Whilst the *Tanach*, which comprises the Five Books of Moses, the Prophets and the Writings, is seen as the fundamental text of the Jews it is the *Gemara* (Talmud) which is the encyclopaedia of interpretation. It is a compendium of dialectic discussion collated, together with early legal texts (*Mishna*), over the hundreds of years following the destruction of the Second Temple in the year 70 CE.

It is called the Babylonian Talmud because although there were still Jews in Jerusalem at that time (and compiled the Jerusalem Talmud), most Jews had been expelled and exiled to Babylon after the destruction of the First Temple in 586 BCE.

The Jews flourished in Babylon even in the wake of the destruction of the First and the Second Temples. The great Academies of learning at Sura and Pumbedita were established there and the Babylonian Talmud was completed around the year 600 CE.

The Gemara uses the spoken language of the time, Aramaic, which is similar to Hebrew and actually written in Hebrew characters. The Gemara consists of some 37 tractates covering every aspect of life from tying shoelaces to the sexual practices of a married couple.

Among the Eastern European (Ashkenazi) Jews, Gemara had been taught using their vernacular language at the time, which was Yiddish (a German dialect) and in Israel the language of instruction was, unsurprisingly, Hebrew.

One of the Diaspora Yeshiva's innovations (brought to Israel from America) was the use of English as the language of instruction.

While the immigrants from Russia, Poland and Eastern Europe spoke Yiddish, as indeed did my parents, even though they had been born in England, most of the next generation spoke only the language of their country and therefore the Gemara had been inaccessible to most modern secular and English speaking Jews.

Following the Six-Day War in Israel, with the influx of Jewish youth as volunteers and the greater opportunities generally for travel to the Holy Land, the spell was broken and, by 1973, the Talmud had become accessible to English speaking college kids, and indeed me at the age of 26.

Karen studied at the Womens' College. This itself was an innovation as most religious women at that time were educated to a poor secondary school standard just about sufficient to enable them to run a home. An institution devoted to the higher education of women was revolutionary.

Meanwhile, at a governmental level there was a lot of red tape to get into the Israeli system, more so because we had not made any arrangements before immigrating but had done so spontaneously.

After many weeks of hassle and form filling, the Jewish Agency finally accepted our applications and The State of Israel granted us A1 temporary resident status.

Hevenu Shalom Aleichem

(Hebrew Folk Song)

The period from 1973 to 1978, when we lived in Jerusalem, is difficult to write about. It was, on the one hand, one of the happiest periods of our married life, but on the other hand, at specific times, it was filled with tension.

Seeking spirituality, we had found religion which is not necessarily the same thing. To be fair we had also found a community of like-minded people, mostly Americans, who were generally more open to these things in the 1970s than their British counterparts.

So, broadly speaking, we were middle-class hippies seeking spiritual truth and we chose to do this by rediscovering our roots.

Israel is a country that welcomes and encourages Jewish immigration and making aliyah (emigrating to Israel) is, for most new immigrants, a well-thought-out process involving disposing of property, consolidating assets, shipping furniture and negotiating with various authorities to acquire the proper documentation.

We had no real assets, so our aliyah consisted of packing a trunk and hopping on a plane with a few hundred pounds in our pockets.

Nevertheless, and despite our unconventional approach, after around three months of being in the country, living in Geula with Mrs Levy, and going to a yeshiva (Rabbinical College) we had fallen into a seriously religious lifestyle.

We were then allocated a brand new rental apartment, by the Jewish agency, which fitted that lifestyle.

The apartment was in a district called Sanhedria Hamurchevet and we lived there for the next year or so.

This was a new neighbourhood which had been built on the northern outskirts of Jerusalem as an extension of an older district located near the original site of the tombs of the elders of the Sanhedrin. The Sanhedrin was the highest legal court in the era of the Second Temple, 2000 years ago.

The apartment building was on a sloping site so, to reach our front door, we had to go down one flight of stairs, but from the living room and the balcony, we had the most spectacular view of the Judean Hills.

The area was populated in the main by very religious families, many of whom were Jewish American immigrants, but there were quite a number of secular Israeli families also living there. For the most part the community rubbed along very well. The area was designed around an access road in the shape of a horseshoe and the whole neighbourhood could therefore be easily closed off from vehicular traffic on the Sabbath.

Years later, sadly, the community became socially polarised, the secular families moved out and the area became virtually one hundred per cent religious.

Shortly after we moved into our new apartment the Yom Kippur War broke out.

KOL NIDRE

(Opening Prayer of Yom Kippur)

Yom Kippur, the Day of Atonement, is the holiest day in the Jewish calendar and is a nil-by-mouth fast of 25 hours. No food, no drink, no smoking. The whole day is spent in the synagogue, praying.

This year Yom Kippur had fallen on a Saturday, but since Yom Kippur is a fast day ordained in the written scripture even the Holy Sabbath, usually a day of food and drink, is superceded.

The seriously religious people of Sanhedria did not have televisions but while they did have radios on this day of days, all electrical appliances are switched off to allow concentration on prayer.

To our cousins, the sons of Ishmael, our religious devotion on Yom Kippur is well known and so it was on this day, that they launched a massive invasion, with the Egyptian forces crossing the Suez Canal to begin an advance through Sinai. At the same time the Syrians attacked from the north.

To those interested in the Yom Kippur war, much has been written but the subject is not within the scope of this book. Suffice it to say that as Egypt came up from the south and Syrian troops attempted to regain control of the Golan Heights from the north, so the news filtered through to us, fasting and praying for forgiveness and redemption in a simple synagogue building on the outskirts of Jerusalem.

Slowly, as word spread, the general mobilization began, and reserve soldiers left the synagogue. The true implication of this existential war began to sink in, that once again the Arabs would try to push the Jews into the sea.

The reality dawned on the population of Israel that on 6 October 1973, the Egyptian army had achieved the unthinkable and smashed through the Bar Lev line, with access to Sinai, and the Syrians were close to achieving their goal to overrun the Galilee.

Ironically, even though the Arabs may have thought that Israel would be hampered by the fact that it was Yom Kippur, in fact the general mobilisation was easier to effect, because most reservists were either at home or in the synagogue, so that their whereabouts were known.

In 19 days of fierce fighting the Israel Defence Forces halted the advance of the Egyptians, and in a brilliant strategy, General Ariel Sharon leading his troops, crossed over the Suez canal reaching the town of Suez, and surrounded the Egyptian Third Army. The Israelis then pushed back the Syrians to within striking distance of Damascus.

By the 25 October there was a ceasefire leaving Israel in a commanding position, but the Israeli casualties were very heavy. Two and a half thousand dead and eight thousand wounded.

Son Of My Right Hand

(Jacob the Prophet)

It was while living in Sanhedria, on Friday night, 29 Adar 5734 (22 March 1974) that Karen went into labour.

Since it was the Sabbath, the barriers to the neighbourhood were moved to allow access for an ambulance. (In the Jewish religion, a woman in labour is considered to be in a life-threatening situation and therefore many of the Sabbath restrictions do not apply.)

Eighteen hours later, in Hadassah Hospital, Ein Kerem, my dear wife gave birth to our first son. Although I planned to be at the birth, because of the long labour, and the cord being tangled up, I was chucked out of the delivery room at the last minute.

In many ways our first son represented our *Aliyah* to the Land of Israel and our return to the ways of our ancestors and so we named him Binyamin (Benjamin – 'son of the right hand') after the tribe of that name and youngest son of the patriarch Jacob, which, over three thousand years earlier had been allocated the area containing Jerusalem, our home.

Karen was discharged after a few days but Ben (as he is now known) had caught a slight infection in the hospital and was kept in for a further 10 days.

Accordingly his *brit* (circumcision), which was delayed by one day, was performed at the hospital. The *mohel* (circumciser) was a *Chassid* named Reb Weisberg who was considered a somewhat strange character, not least because he drove a white Volkswagen. He was known in Jerusalem as the 'fastest blade in the East'.

When Ben was discharged, Karen put him in a baby sling and we took him home on his first bus ride from Ein Kerem, the village outside of Jerusalem, where the hospital is located.

'Karen, Ben and me in Jerusalem 1975'

AMIDAR

(An Israeli government housing agency)

We had moved into our new apartment with an immigration pack which consisted of two iron bedsteads, mattresses, pillows, and blankets, some pots and pans, and a paraffin camping stove to cook on.

After some months, Amidar, the construction company which represented the Jewish Agency offered all the new tenants the opportunity to buy their apartments with a concessionary government mortgage. All that was needed was a $10,000 down payment.

Needless to say, we did not have the down payment as we were really living from hand to mouth. Our neighbours, who were all taking up the opportunity, could not understand why we were not buying our apartment. Most of them were Americans, also studying, but receiving support money from their families back home.

During this time, our new found friends and colleagues at the Diaspora Yeshiva, and indeed the Rabbi, had convinced us to immerse ourselves in study and not to worry about money. The prevailing concept was that, at least from a spiritual point of view, if we did the right thing and devoted ourselves to religious study and did God's commandments, in some miraculous way money would be provided and we would survive. Of course, most of the people giving the advice also received money from their parents and families back home.

Nevertheless miracles did occur at some levels. The first was getting even a rental apartment in Sanhedria

Murchevet, although this miracle was implemented through the auspices of a government department, the Jewish Agency.

A further miracle occurred by a slight manipulation of the system of benefits received by new immigrants. I am not proud of my actions in this respect but, at the time, I did not have many options.

When we took the apartment we had no fridge, we cooked on a camping stove and we had no washing machine. Our son had just been born and we lived in an era of terry towel nappies, which Karen washed by hand. Although disposable nappies had been invented they were prohibitively expensive.

Things were pretty difficult and so, by selling our rights to import certain luxury goods tax free, which were much sought after in Israel, we received in exchange similar Israeli products of lesser quality.

In that way we were able to obtain white goods for the apartment, a fridge freezer, a gas range to cook on, and crucially a washing machine.

At this juncture, I hear you scream, why didn't you get a job? Good question.

Meanwhile, our neighbours had decided that they could not let us miss the opportunity of buying our apartment, so they grouped together and offered to lend us the down payment on the apartment. Another miracle?

I was reluctant to take the money because in truth I could not see how we were going to be able to pay the money back, but these good people insisted on providing a loan with no interest on a 'pay it back when you can' basis.

We accepted and bought the apartment.

Meanwhile, by some fluke I had progressed in my studies and had been accepted as a member of the Kollel. In a yeshiva, members of the Kollel are the advanced married scholars, who undertake higher rabbinical studies, and while I had only been in the yeshiva for a very short time, nevertheless, I took to the dialectic arguments of the Babylonian Talmud like the proverbial fish to water. While my language skills were never good enough to get me to the top Shiur (class) I did manage to cope reasonably well at the next level down.

The next miracle, which at least happened within the environs of a religious institution, was the fact that, as a member of the Kollel, I received a nominal, but still welcome, monthly stipend. I was being paid to study.

All this does not detract from the fact that you were right... I needed a job.

To continue, I should give the reader some background information, part of which I have already covered.

I had grown up in Southend-on-Sea close to the Rubin family, that is David, Bernard and their sister Belle.

David had come to Israel first, and his brother, my best friend Bernard, had married an Australian girl and would ultimately end up in Australia.

Their sister, Belle, was a dear friend of mine and back in the day we'd even dated a couple of times. When Karen came to England she and Belle became very close friends and then Belle also immigrated to Israel. She married an Israeli, Yachin, and they lived on the outskirts of Jerusalem and had four children.

At one point, Belle had a job as a secretary to a research Professor at Hadassah hospital where Ben had been born. She told me that he was looking for an assistant in the laboratory, and so I became a part time research assistant at the hospital, but still continued my studies.

My job was feeding rats. Not my favourite animal it has to be said, but I nurtured them from birth and fed them a diet which included copious amounts of sugar as, essentially, the idea was to see whether the rats developed diabetes because, at that time, there was a medical hypothesis that sugar caused the disease.

Israel, of course, is a leader in medical science but the research in this particular laboratory succeeded only to the extent that they proved that sugar, in fact, does not cause diabetes. I like to think that I contributed to that medical breakthrough.

So there we were, in less than a year we had established ourselves as a religious couple, studying and working in Jerusalem, owning a fitted apartment and blessed with a wonderful baby boy.

THE GREEN LINE

(Ceasefire Line following the War of Independence 1948)

The aspirations of most of the members of the Kollel included the possibility that they could at some time live as a community on *Har Zion* (Mount Zion). And plans were afoot to move married couples onto the mountain.

Prior to this, the president of the yeshiva, Rabbi Dr S. Z. Kahane, had allowed only single yeshiva boys to live in the old Crusader buildings which surrounded King David's tomb.

Dr Kahane's claim emanated from the success of the Six-Day War in 1967 when the then Minister of Defense, Moshe Dayan, gave him control of the area which had previously been in an area of no man's land between Israel and Jordan and over the Ceasefire Line following the War of Independence. This was because Dr Kahane was, at that time, Director General of the Ministry of Religious Affairs.

The problem was that not only was this a particularly sensitive issue because of the international political dimension but Dr Kahane had not previously wanted a confrontation with the Israel Lands Authority, who after 1967 had themselves claimed administrative control of the mountain.

However, by 1975, Dr Kahana had finally decided that the time was right. There were some buildings a little way down the mountain, which had included the yeshiva dining room and it was agreed that these various ramshackle buildings could be converted to house around six families.

Meanwhile, the loan that I taken from my kind neighbours to buy our apartment was weighing on my mind. How would I ever pay it back? Fortunately, the apartment had risen in value and we had built up an equity in it.

I decided that the only way I could pay back the apartment loan was to sell the apartment, which became an option in the knowledge that we now had another place to live.

One of the jobs in the yeshiva that fell to me was to supervise the building project to convert various shacks and outbuildings into liveable family quarters.

Mussa was a friendly Arab builder from Azaria, a suburb of East Jerusalem, and he was on call to the yeshiva as we were always involved in building work related to opening some long abandoned areas on the mountain. He was a nice man who could do anything or get anything you needed..

So, it came to pass that I worked with Mussa on the new living areas. This consisted of converting existing structures into small habitable units, installing shower units and rudimentary kitchens and connecting different buildings with cement pathways to form a small commune.

We sold the apartment in Sanhedria.

In this way, I was able to pay off the loan from my neighbours and after having given 10% *maaser* money (charitable tithe) to the yeshiva, which was a religious obligation, we had a small amount of money left over.

Now came a major spiritual test.

During that year, my father needed a serious heart operation and I wanted to go to England to be with him. So, I asked my Rabbi, and he said I should go... on my own. My subsequent actions were to define a new spiritual direction for us.

AYECHA

(Genesis – 'Where are you?')

I felt that I could not leave my family at that time, and so I decided that we should all go to England, together.

My father had his heart surgery, recuperated, and we duly returned to Jerusalem. We had been at the yeshiva for two years but from that point onwards our relationship with Rabbi Goldstein had changed.

Outwardly, this change would not have been noticeable. In fact I had somewhat risen through the ranks and I was in Kollel (Advanced Student Group) and studying with the Rabbi in one of the top Talmudic classes.

In 1973, we had come to Israel, to Jerusalem in search of spiritual truth, a search for answers to the perennial philosophical questions – 'Who am I?' and 'Why am I here?'

The concept of God had not really been too much of a problem and, to be honest, any doubts in the existence of a Supreme Being had been somewhat dispelled by our intermittent but various psychedelic experiences at the beginning of the decade.

Also, discovering the nature of God and delving into the mysteries of our joint heritage seemed a very reasonable route to take for a couple of middle-class hippies. God was not the problem, but unquestioning commitment to an earthly leader was.

We had accepted the idea that a seeker needs a leader and indeed this accorded with the exhortation in a Tractate of the Mishnah known as *Pirke Avot* (Ethics of the Fathers), *Aseh Lecha Rav* (Find yourself a Teacher), and we had chosen Rabbi Goldstein.

At the time the question arose as to how you prepare yourself to fully absorb the truth from any spiritual leader and it appears that the biggest obstacle to accepting spiritual truth is your own personality.

This particularly applies to the face that you project to the outside world or perhaps more accurately the way in which you want the world to see you. From a Freudian perspective that would probably be defined as ego.

According to Judaism, in order therefore to truly absorb spiritual truth, humility is the order of the day that is why Moses was described as a 'humble' man, and it was that trait that qualified him to receive the Torah from God.

How do you achieve true humility? Apparently by suppressing the ego. So here is a Word of Torah!

And the Lord God called to the man (in the Garden of Eden) and said to him *"Ayecha"* which is usually translated in Genesis as 'Where are you…?' Actually the Hebrew word is the same word as the first word of the Book of Lamentations which there is translated 'How… (deserted lies the city)'

So, God was not asking Adam, 'Where are you?' in the conventional sense, because obviously God knew spatially where Adam was. God was asking Adam 'where' in the sense of the Americanism 'where are you holding?' i.e. 'how are you?' That is 'emotionally', because it is in the world of the higher emotions that man experiences the divine, and so the Eternal One asks *'Where are you in relation to me?'*

110

As a single guy I had pretty much made my own decisions in life. Now I was 26 years old and married with a child. Karen had her own mind and was a huge influence on whatever decision making process took place in my brain, as indeed I was on hers.

But, in not taking the Rabbi's advice (and going to England as a family), we were, as one, rejecting the advice, albeit advice of a temporal nature, of our spiritual leader.

Still the yeshiva was not a cult, and therefore this subtle shift in emphasis did not change our day to day activities.

The Well Of Miriam

(Midrash)

By 1975, we were living on Mount Zion.

As mentioned, for 19 years prior, most of Mount Zion had been an area of no man's land between the State of Israel and the Hashemite Kingdom of Jordan, and the buildings on the mountain had been abandoned.

Since we were on the Green Line in a politically sensitive location I had to undertake basic training and became a civil guard attached to the police.

I had supervised Mussa the Arab contractor in the rebuilding of a gated area on the lower part of the mountain and converted some of the abandoned buildings into tiny apartment units.

Karen, myself and our new son, Ben, moved into one of the units which consisted of a main room, a tiny anteroom, kitchen, shower room and WC. Five other married couples moved into the other units.

Karen was pregnant again.

I was a little older than some of my friends in the Kollel. In England, I had started work after leaving secondary school and had been in the workplace for 10 years. By contrast, my fellow students, mostly Americans, had been to college, many of them had never had a real job and most of them received allowances from their parents.

It was true that they were committed to living a spiritual life. They knew how to devote themselves to learning and they would spend many waking hours in study, some a little more than others, but they all had one thing in common, and that was an aversion to physical work.

It soon became clear that my aspirations for the small compound that we had established were at odds with theirs. My vision was a neat and tidy group of apartments, painted white and set in a tailored landscape with kibbutz style green lawns, copiously watered by irrigation pipes and sprinklers.

Accordingly, my initial suggestion that we all get together like the early pioneers and remove the stones and rocks from the ground was met with resistance, if not derision. It is easy, when you are busy being spiritual, to claim that you have more important things to do!

Yom HaZicharon in Israel is a memorial day for all the soldiers lost in the wars against the Arab nations. It falls on the fourth day of the month of Iyar which is the day before Israel's Independence Day and is marked by the sounding of a siren in middle of the day.

On *Yom HaZicharon* 5736 (4 May 1976) we were outside King David's Tomb at the bottom of the stairs leading to the Coenaculum (the room where Jesus was reputed to have held The Last Supper) when the siren went off.

Everyone stood stock still, and... Karen went into labour.

Our friend Elliot drove us to Hadassah hospital and Karen was taken straight to the delivery room where she was having regular contractions.

I was called out of the delivery room by a nurse who said that some visitors had arrived! Our aunt and uncle from England had chosen that very day to visit us and, having been told we had gone to the hospital, had followed us there.

It was about 40 minutes after we had arrived at the hospital and in the moment that I left to tell our visitors that this was not the most convenient time to visit... my first daughter was born. Once again I missed the birth.

We named her Miriam after Karen's mother. The name in Hebrew contains the word for water and the tradition is that the prophetess Miriam provided water for the Congregation of Israel when they wandered in the desert.

THE INGATHERING
OF THE EXILES

(from Deuteronomy 30:1–5)

There was, and still is, an international religious and political dimension to the area known as Mount Zion in Jerusalem.

At the time we were there, the former director general of the Ministry of Religious Affairs, Dr Kahane claimed control of much of the mountain, including the Tomb of King David because he had been given that responsibility in 1967 by the Defense Minister, Moshe Dayan. Many of the buildings had been abandoned because, although the Tomb was on the Israeli side, the eastern frontage had previously been right on the ceasefire line and within the sights of Jordanian snipers.

The Tomb itself is venerated by Muslims, a number of buildings on the mountain are occupied by different sects of the Christian faith including the monks of the German Dormition Abbey and the Greek Orthodox Church. The upper part of the Tomb consists of the Cenacle or Coenaculam and is considered to be the Room of the Last Supper and therefore the place associated with the formation of the early Christian church.

Many of the buildings were constructed in the Crusader period just before the conquest of Jerusalem by Saladin in the early 12th century. After 1967, when Israel occupied the mountain, Dr Kahane established a Holocaust memorial museum and many of the buildings were handed to the Diaspora Yeshiva to progress his vision of the 'ingathering of the exiles'. Ultimately, of course, the land is controlled by the Israel Lands Authority but it suited them to allow the yeshiva to occupy many of the previously abandoned buildings to encourage a Jewish presence on the mountain.

Three years had passed since Karen and I had arrived in Israel and we were now living on Mount Zion as part the Diaspora Yeshiva in what was considered by many to be a somewhat fanatical community of religious ex-hippies in thrall to an American Rabbi. Our living quarters consisted of two miniscule rooms, with Ben sleeping in a tiny anteroom, Karen and I sleeping in the main room, and little Miriam occupying a cot next to our bed.

The money that we had accumulated from the sale of our previous apartment had virtually gone and although I was getting some money as a stipend we were not making ends meet. After a few months, we had become quite depressed, particularly as the physical ambience around the living quarters had not developed in the way we had expected.

It is true that we were living in a unique and holy place, minutes from the Western Wall of the Second Temple, but from another more cynical perspective the place just consisted of some ramshackle buildings on a dusty mountainside which quickly turned into a muddy area when it rained. At a spiritual level, also, we were drifting away as the reality of the situation sank in and the choices became apparent... either we had to come to terms with a life of abject poverty in an area that was rapidly becoming a slum or we had to abandon ship.

With trepidation we chose the latter.

That is not to say that we gave up our spiritual search, after all we had made our way to Jerusalem, but we decided to continue our journey within the context of a more conventional lifestyle. The challenge was to find a new home and a way to generate some income.

I told the Rabbi that, as a family, we needed to leave. He accepted our decision but wanted us to retain a connection with the community. Knowing that I had been working as a professional in England and that I had a grip on business affairs he offered me a job as an executive director of the yeshiva, with responsibilities, (together with others) for fundraising, cultural activities, general administration and liaison with our president Rabbi Dr S.Z. Kahane.

On fundraising I worked with Danny Schultz, Elliott Sherman and David Rubin. On the cultural side I worked with Avraham Rosenblum, who in a previous life had been a rock guitarist but by then was the leader of the Diaspora Yeshiva Band. All of these characters were to ultimately receive their rabbinical qualifications in one form or another and indeed even I was given the title in an approbation by Rabbi Dr S. Z. Kahane.

At one point I also became the manager of the band which would become the best known Jewish rock band, headlining with other famous artists of the day such as Shlomo Carlebach.

I worked closely with Rabbi Mordechai Alexander on the administrative side of things. Mordechai was not specifically a disciple of Rabbi Goldstein but was happy to work with him and advance the interests of the yeshiva. He had received rabbinical Semicha (ordination) from the great Illui (genius) Rabbi Chaim Zimmerman, whose magnum opus was a book on the significance of

117

the international dateline in Jewish Law (this was roughly the Jewish equivalent of *A Brief History of Time* by Stephen Hawking, at least to the uninitiated).

On the living front, we moved to an apartment in a good part of town and, for a time, life was pretty exciting, as, after all we were at the forefront of a new movement and part of an illustrious group of Baa'lei Teshuva Yeshivot which included Ohr Sameach, Aish HaTorah and Dvar Yerushalayim.

By 1976 the Diaspora Yeshiva had a community of over 200 souls, comprising single male students living on the mountain, a girl's school in the Jewish Quarter of the Old City and a Kollel of about 15 families living on the mountain and in the town.

The yeshiva was becoming a sizable institution. I opened a new bank account for the yeshiva at the American Israel Bank and had to wrest control of the finances from the Rabbi's wife. She is in many ways a remarkable and formidable woman, who produced 13 children and still had time to run the finances of the nascent institution from her handbag, until I came along.

During this period, I went to England fundraising and travelled across North America with Avraham Rosenblum to set up the first tour of the Diaspora Yeshiva Band. Our scouting trip included a visit to the Concorde Hotel in the Catskills in the middle of winter to present a Super 8 movie of the band to a group of Israeli emissaries.

The yeshiva, however, was never far from controversy.

Our legal case against the Israel Lands Authority reached the Supreme Court and I spent much of the time with lawyers fighting the case. Ironically, one of the partners of the law firm that represented us, was the husband of Dorit Beinisch who many years later became president of the Supreme Court.

There were confrontations with various factions on the mountain including the American Institute of Holy Land Studies which claimed part of our campus as their own.

As regard to cultural activities, visitors to King David's Tomb had to be entertained and we also ran a club known as Assaf's Cave for tourists, which provided entertainment in the form of Druze dancing. The Saturday night Malave Malka concerts which we promoted on the mountain were renowned in Jerusalem and were always oversubscribed, and on occasion reached an attendance level of up to 1,000 young people who loved the idea of such a new wave religious event.

All this is to say nothing of the reaction of the mainstream religious communities of Jerusalem, the *Charedim* ('those with the fear of God') were apoplectic at this bunch of hippies purporting to be religious, and taking centre stage in the religious life of the Holy City.

One evening I was walking on the mountain alone when the pressure of work overwhelmed me. I was so overcome by stress and the level of responsibility that my head felt like it was going to explode. I staggered around for quite a while trying consolidate my thoughts through a massive and pounding migraine.

After a while, I recalled that one of the students, an American guy called Lazer, was a gentle soul and had a reputation as an alternative healer. I went to his room which was high in the complex of Crusader buildings surrounding King David's tomb and knocked on his door.

Lazer told me to come in and sit down. I explained how I felt and he proceeded to massage my neck and head for the next two hours. Later he gave me some herbal tea and let me lie down on his bed. I slowly recovered that evening but knew, in my heart of hearts, that my days working at the Diaspora Yeshiva were over.

Topsy Turvy

(Children's Hair Salon)

Karen had operated a small business while we had been living in Sanhedria, which consisted of styling wigs for the religious women in the area who, as married women, were obliged to cover their hair. A number of the women had asked her to cut their children's hair and we hit upon the idea of opening a children's hairdressing shop in town. I found a perfect ground floor commercial property to rent in the centre of Jerusalem right behind the *Mashbir* department store.

I went to see my Arab friend, Mr Bazian, who owned a scrap yard out by Jerusalem airport and could source or make anything. I had him make up some small leather high chairs for kids, and he supplied large mirrors and an aquarium for the premises. Yehudit, the wife of one of our friends had, in a previous life, been a receptionist in a beauty salon, so she joined as Karen's assistant and we called the shop 'Topsy Turvy'.

The shop was advertised and customers started to arrive… but disaster struck.

About a week or so after opening the shop Karen caught pneumonia and was laid up in the apartment, unable to move. The fever was so high that she was hallucinating.

I called Yehuda Schupack, who had been our doctor when we lived in Sanhedria and he was an old-school doctor originally from Belgium. He diagnosed viral pneumonia but told us that, under no circumstances was I to take Karen to hospital. His reasoning was that since it was viral pneumonia there were no drugs which could be effective and the hospital would just give Karen large doses of antibiotics, which would probably make her susceptible to secondary infection.

He insisted that he would treat her at home, with very high doses of aspirin to bring down the fever, and copious quantities of liquid orange juice supplement. It took nearly three months for her to fully recover.

So for those three months I would take the kids to the kindergarten in the morning and stay with Karen all day until it was time to pick up the kids. The doctor came every couple of days to check on her, and she slowly recovered.... after that, Karen was in no condition to run a business and we had to close the shop even though Yehudit had tried valiantly to keep it open.

I now considered getting a job, however, my conversational skills in Hebrew were limited. Even though I had been studying ancient biblical texts, these tended to be in Aramaic, concentrating on the deep meaning of a few words at a time, in the lilting style of the Babylonian Talmud... and also since there had been much other stuff to learn including prayers and religious observances, Hebrew as a spoken language had not been high on the list of priorities. Hebrew as a language was very neglected in the yeshiva, if not actually discouraged.

I did, however, still have the contract on the shop, and in considering other businesses that I could run from the premises I hit upon the idea of a language school. You may think this a little ironic considering my own language skills but not so if you follow a certain logic. If I needed to learn the language there must have been others in the same position!

Meanwhile, we were not the only ones that had become disillusioned with the yeshiva. At various times other alumni would leave, some retaining links with the place, others making a complete break. One friend of mine, who had left the yeshiva was a brilliant linguist and I proposed that we become partners – he would write a Hebrew language course and I would deal with the administration.

So, back to Mr Bazian, who supplied study chairs and blackboards and transformed the premises into a school.

The International Language Center was born at No 7 Mesillat Yesharim Street, as advertised in the *Jerusalem Post*. It took a while to get going but the courses ran, people paid and they learned Hebrew. We expanded to run English as a foreign language.

I knew that the school would only provide a limited income for my partner and myself, so while the school was running, I started to think of other business ideas.

I banked at a small private bank known as Otzar Hitsachon and had a good relationship with them. In fact, at one point the manager had asked me if I new anyone who needed a job as a cashier, so I introduced another disaffected student from the yeshiva who subsequently worked at the bank for a number of years before returning to Canada.

The manager was impressed with my various business ideas and agreed to give me a personal overdraft of $5,000 which kept us going for a while and also enabled me to fund my partner in the language school, who also had no money.

HOPE SPRINGS ETERNAL

(Alexander Pope)

I was establishing a business relationship with the contractor Mussa's brother, Ibrahim who was a successful businessman from East Jerusalem.

Jerusalem had been annexed by Israel in 1967, and the barbed wire and divisions that separated the Old City from the Western half of Jerusalem were removed.

Initially, both the Jordanian Arabs and Israeli Jews were fascinated by each other's lives and, in the period after the war, the populations mixed freely to discover how the other half lived.

Even after the Yom Kippur War in 1973, it was not unusual for Jews to be seen in Salah Al Din Street in East Jerusalem, and since Jews now had access to the Western Wall they would often be seen walking through the Souk to get to that part of the Old City. By the same token Arabs from East Jerusalem now had access to the shops in Jaffa Road and the Western part of the city.

Ibrahim and I became friends and discussed many business ideas of which the main one was the potential export of steel to Jordan. At that time farmers in Jordan used cloches to protect crops from cold weather and these protective covers were supported by simple steel rods which were bent into shape and stuck in the earth. The farmers in Jordan could not obtain sufficient quantity of the steel rods and they were very expensive in Jordan.

Israel had a large steel works in Haifa and there was a trade in steel rods that were being bought cheaply in Israel and smuggled across the Allenby Bridge into Jordan.

Politically, although there was a ceasefire, there was no peace treaty at that time with Jordan and so Israel could not officially supply Jordan. However, from the Israeli point of view there was no reason why a third country could not ship goods to the port of Aqaba in Jordan.

In 1967, Jerusalem had been re-unified, and the Arab population had become permanent residents of Israel (with the option of Israeli citizenship) while retaining their Jordanian passports.

Ibrahim convinced me that he could easily obtain orders for the steel from Jordan and so we worked together on a business plan. I set up a company with offices in New York, the idea being that orders would be made through the US, the steel bought at Haifa and shipped to Aqaba.

I had great hopes for the new business idea and Ibrahim insisted there was a tremendous demand from Jordan.

Needless to say, and to cut a very long story short, we did not manage to pull it off.

The best laid plans of mice and men...

Ultimately, the truth sank in. The only way I would be able to support my growing family going forward, was to live in a place where I could earn sufficient money by working in an industry that I knew well.

And so it was in late 1978, that our first Israel adventure ended and reluctantly we returned to England.

Rivers Of Babylon

(Boney M)

It was November 1978 when we returned to England and I was determined to re-establish myself in London. I contacted an old friend, Alan Sharr, who was a partner at a property agency in London called Garrard Smith & Partners and, based on my previous experience, he gave me a job working as an office negotiator.

Initially, we rented a flat in my old hometown of Southend and put the kids in a small school that had been established in the building that had housed my childhood Hebrew classes next to the synagogue in Westcliff-on-Sea. Every day Karen would walk to the school and back again with Miriam snuggled up in a pushchair and Ben at her side. It was a particularly severe winter that year and this journey was often made through driving snow.

A few months later I moved the family to a small rented flat in Belsize Park in London and enrolled the kids into a Jewish School in Willesden. Living in London, and with two kids, we needed transport, so with the job Alan threw in an old Citroen DS that he owned and also I bought an old banger for Karen so that she could collect the kids from school.

By then we had toned down our religious observance. Karen no longer covered her hair and I did not wear a *kippa* (skullcap) all the time, but we still considered ourselves 'religious', duly observing the Sabbath and Festivals and eating kosher.

Fortunately, the flat was located opposite a Grodzinski Kosher Bakery so one problem was solved. In 1978, most regular processed bread in England was not kosher, often containing whale oil and lard. Nowadays, largely because of the end of commercial whaling and health considerations most processed bread no longer contains these ingredients. Also as a result of European regulations these days you can tell much more accurately what is contained in most processed foods, including bread.

In reality, the rented flat was too small, so after some months and with the help of my company and a 100% mortgage we bought a dilapidated two bedroom flat on the third floor of a building looked after by our management department. Morshead Mansions was, and still is, quite a well known block in Maida Vale, and it was close enough to the school in Willesden that we did not have to move the kids again.

These days an apartment in Morshead is considered to be quite fashionable, but at that time it was pretty shabby and had no lift, and having to drag a pushchair up three flights of stairs was not all that convenient. Still, it was our first real family home since returning to England. It was here that Karen became pregnant again and on 19 October, 1979, our darling Sarah was born at the Royal Free hospital in Hampstead.

For the next couple of years I kept my head down and got back into the swing of commercial real estate in London.

Just around the corner from the office was a small vegetarian restaurant called the 'Raw Deal' and virtually every day I would have lunch there with a group of property guys, agents, surveyors, and developers. Most of us would arrive late in order to miss the early lunch crowd and we could often be found there in the late afternoon talking real estate over coffee and desert.

It was at the Raw Deal that I met my dear late friend Brian Norman. Brian was a chartered surveyor and in his earlier years had been a partner of the famous property agency Conrad Ritblat run by Sir John Ritblat who later became head of British Land. Brian was superfit, running every day and playing squash twice a week and later was to become became a consultant to my own agency. We were firm friends up until his tragic demise at the age of 52 years.

The senior partner of Garrard Smith was David Garrard (now Sir David) and our staff meetings were legendary. Much of the time at these meetings was spent on administrative matters with DG often berating staff members with particular attention to such important details as lack of toilet paper in the executive WC on the ground floor. Tim the office junior got more than his fair share of criticism.

The WC on the ground floor was the executive suite. We knew this was the executive suite because it was clean, tiled and in a nod to bad taste had a telephone installed specifically for DG's use (this was before the era of mobile phones). The only other toilet facility was a dirty outside WC for the staff, located at the inner well of the building at basement level.

A client of ours, Firestone Tire Company, was at that time the second largest company in the world and by a quirk of fate our company was selling their main UK property the famous Firestone Tire Factory in Brentford.

On one occasion the executives of Firestone were flying in from the States for a meeting at our modest little office building in Crawford Street.

Nature, of course, has a way of levelling the most important of our species and so it came about that a large black limo pulled up outside our offices, the chauffeur ran round to the passenger side and the president of Firestone jumped out, desperate to go to the loo.

He was directed to the executive WC but it was occupied and so, horror of horrors, our biggest client had to visit the outside toilet in the basement.

He came up the stairs from the basement with a strange startled look on his face as if to say, 'I have just been back in time to the world of Charles Dickens.'

We were all mortified, and the more so when the door of the executive loo opened and Tim, the office junior appeared, having been on the telephone to a recruitment agency trying to get another job!

After a couple of years with Garrard Smith I received a call from Kenneth Brown, who had been my old boss well before we had left for Israel.

He had heard that I was back in town and offered me a great job to run his new office at £9,000 a year plus commission, and a new Ford.

Had he completely forgotten that he had fired me 15 years earlier? I never asked him, but took the job anyway. The new office was located in a period house in Brook Street, Mayfair.

Twenty-five Brook Street was the house where the famous composer George Frederick Handel lived from 1723, and it was later turned into Handel's Museum in London.

During the late 1960s a friend of mine had opened a restaurant next door at No 23 Brook Street called 'Mr Love', and Jimi Hendricks lived in the flat above the restaurant.

So, there I was, negotiating real estate deals on the very spot where Handel composed many of his famous operas and next door to where Jimi Hendricks lived.

What a claim to fame!

The Old Hall

(Part of the Arundel Estate)

With a wife and three kids, getting ahead was not easy and somehow my wages never quite seemed to cover my expenses. However, at least there had been an increase in property values and so we decided to take advantage of the rise, and sell the flat.

I calculated that after settling various debts we would have just about £4,000 profit left over and I started to look for a rental property.

It was then that I saw a private advertisement in *The Times* advertising a luxury flat in Highgate.

The apartment was one of several residential units carved out of a fabulous mansion house in Highgate Village. The house was built in 1691 on the site of an original house dating from the 16th century and is a Grade II listed property.

Later the house was to be purchased and restored by Terry Gilliam, the film director, of Monty Python fame and his wife, Maggie.

The flat had three bedrooms, and was situated in the ground floor of the east wing of the house. It contained a magnificent panelled room of about 350 sq ft and a patio leading out to a two acre mature garden.

For legal reasons the owner could only rent the flat to a limited company and the quoted rent was £100 per week. Fortunately, I had at that time, and after some wishful thinking, just incorporated a company (which had no assets) and I decided to offer the owner all of the

£4,000 up front for the first year with an option to renew for a second year.

He accepted and so began the residency of Mr and Mrs D. Lewis (recently returned from a lengthy spiritual sojourn in the Middle East) together with their three lovely children at – The Old Hall, Highgate Village, London, N6.

The time that we lived at the Old Hall was good. Our play area was a two acre mature garden, beautifully tended by professional landscape gardeners and even open to the public once a year. I say 'our' play area because the kids effectively had their own park with a gentle slope, enabling us to lay out a waterslide in the summer. In the winter it was a snowy wonderland. For the adults, our ground floor flat led out on to a flagstone patio for barbecues and entertaining.

We were in the east wing and the west wing of the house was occupied by Mr and Mrs Chris Fenwick part of the family who owned the famous Fenwick Store in Bond Street. They were perfectly correct but we did not socialize with them as they did not have children themselves and were rather too concerned that children did not play on their side of the garden.

Our other neighbours, who had the apartment in the centre of the house, were the McCormicks, an American couple who also had three small children. Jim worked for the Chicago Illinois Bank. The second floor apartment was occupied by the Gudeons. Ed was an American immigration lawyer married to Nicole, and they had two daughters. There was a very nice older couple who lived on the first floor.

During those two years at the Old Hall we did have a number of memorable get togethers, including joint barbeques, at which a special section of the grill was always reserved for our kosher meat.

At the end of the last year, the McCormicks had a Christmas party where strangely we met up with one of our relatives. It turned out that our aunt's sister was there with her husband who worked with Jim at the Chicago Illinois Bank. Small world.

Moving And Shaking

(English expression)

I did not do enough business at Kenneth Brown and he fired me… again, just as he had done 15 years earlier in 1965.

So it was, while were living at the Old Hall, that I started on my own as a commercial agent, working from the end of our bed. Later, I rented an office in Old Bond Street and registered the business name 'Derek Lewis Associates' and my friend Brian Norman became my consultant surveyor.

I had become quite friendly with Peter Galan who was one of the parents at our kids' school in Willesden. He had formerly been a director of Amalgamated Estates, a public company run by property giant Gabriel Harrison which had collapsed in the secondary banking crash of the 1970s. Peter had become an agent, and one of the first agency deals I did with him was the acquisition of the Chubb Lock building in Whitfield Street, W1, for clients.

While Peter and I were waiting to be paid our fees, I came across an opportunity to buy an office building for myself, as a principal. The property, at 25 Newman Street, W1, was a multi-tenanted office building in the West End, whose tenants included John Coletta, manager of the heavy metal band, Deep Purple, with whom I became quite friendly.

I had agreed with the owners to buy the head lease of the building with finance from the National Westminster bank. At the very last minute, when we were just about to exchange contracts, the owners insisted on an extra £5,000, which I did not have.

Fortunately, Peter had received our commission from the deal at Whitfield Street and I contacted him just before he went away for a two week vacation. I rushed over to his house in the evening to collect a cheque and was able to exchange contracts the next day on my first commercial property acquisition as a principal.

I spent the next few months managing and refurbishing the building and then, a while later, I agreed to sell the property to my friend Nick of North Square Properties. The price represented a significant profit.

I was pretty excited about the sale, and had promised Nick that if he actually exchanged contracts to buy the property, Karen and I would take him and his wife for dinner to a restaurant that I had vaguely heard of called Le Gavroche.

Actually, I was being very flash and did not really know Le Gavroche and had certainly never eaten there.

Nick exchanged contracts and insisted that I kept my promise. When I found out that it was one of the only restaurants in London with two Michelin stars, I was somewhat worried that I would not have sufficient money in my pocket on the evening in question and so I took £500 cash out of the bank for the occasion. I only just had enough. This is to say nothing of the challenge of finding food to fit a kosher diet.

By this point in our lives, the kids were growing up fast so we decided that we needed a more conventional lifestyle and fortunately the profit on Newman Street produced enough money to enable us to make a down payment on a house.

Accordingly, we bought a house in a suburb of North London, which was suitably close to one of the big synagogues. The house in Hurstwood Road, Temple Fortune was to become the family home for the next 15 years.

We installed a new kosher kitchen with two sinks and dishwashers for both meat and milk and created a large pergola on the patio which doubled as a frame for a large outside tabernacle ready for the autumn festival of *Sukkoth*.

The house had a through lounge/diner which was a must for Jewish family entertainment and we painted the reception rooms a subtle green, with soft furnishings in shades of dusty pink. These were the distinctive colours of the foliage and houses in Marrakesh, and a nod to a previous life.

By now, on the business front, I had merged my activities into a firm called Whitehouse Lewis which was a three man property agency working out of offices in Devonshire Street.

We expanded the agency representing such clients as the late Christina Onassis and managing such high-profile London apartment blocks as Welbeck House and Biddulph Mansions.

At the same time I expanded my property development activities, by buying old houses in the North London area with money provided by various investors and converting them into prestige flats and apartments. After a while my agency partners, not unreasonably, were concerned that I was not spending enough time on the agency side of things and they bought me out of the partnership.

I needed a new office to continue my activities. There was a small retail shop unit for rent on the ground floor of the office building in which we worked, so I took a lease and opened up a residential estate office.

I named the agency Devonshire Estates fully expecting a nasty letter from the Duke of Devonshire, who owned one of great landed estates in the area, known as the 'Devonshire Estate' but apparently he did not consider that I was competition!

I continued to run the agency successfully while at the same time continuing my development activities from that base.

You Can't Fight City Hall

(American expression)

One of the reasons I truly loved my wife was that, among her many attributes she was also an adventuress and a rebel.

It was 1983, and we were pregnant again. I say we, because Karen was determined that I should be at the event this time, having missed all the other births, and moreover she had decided to have a home birth.

Home births, of course, were very much frowned upon by the medical profession then, and not much has changed today. Although giving birth in hospital sounds eminently sensible (because there is back up if anything goes wrong) there is a question as to whether this approach is true concern for the mother and child, or more for the convenience of medical authorities who have systemised the birthing process.

The situation is quite different in Holland, for instance, where giving birth is not considered an illness and where there is a large percentage of home births. Karen was much affected by the work of Sheila Kitzinger, who was the guru of the Natural Child Birth movement, together with the famous French obstetrician Michel Odent.

We duly attended Natural Childbirth classes in Hampstead with Melanie, a friend and colleague of a pioneer in the field at that time, Janet Balaskas.

Of course if you want to buck the system then you need to prepare and the first issue was to find a sympathetic midwife. At that time, an organization had been formed calling themselves Radical Midwives. This group had formed because they objected to the practice in hospitals of routinely inducing births by various methods including amniotomy ('breaking the waters') which often speeds up the birth before the mother is naturally ready.

Unfortunately, the Radical Midwives Group was radical in another sense, in that they required a declaration from the mother that if she gave birth to a boy, she would not have the baby circumcised, so... not for us.

Later we were recommended to Olive, who was a lovely midwife, and who empathised with Karen's aspirations, was totally supportive, and agreed to attend a home birth under the auspices of the NHS.

The best laid plans...

The one thing that none of us really thought about was the actual date when Karen was due, which was in August, and, as sure as eggs are eggs, Karen went into labour just when dear Olive was on holiday...

I answered the door when the replacement midwife, Bridie, arrived. She was scowling and it was immediately clear that Bridie did not approve of home birth.

Although completely unnecessary, during an examination of Karen she proceeded to induce the birth by breaking the waters and then declared an emergency, and called an ambulance.

And so, my dear youngest son, Adam, was born at Edgware Hospital on 23 August 1983... by Caesarean section.

As they say in the US, you can't fight City Hall!

'The family at our house in London in 1984'

Oak View

(The family home of F Ashe Lincoln QC, RNVR)

It was 1986 and business was going well, but as anyone in the property field will tell you, you are only as good as your next deal.

I had been offered a potential development site for a new block of flats in Golders Green, a middle class residential district close to where I lived. The site had planning consent for 14 units and the price was £1m.

The land consisted of half an acre of open ground surrounding a dilapidated and unremarkable old Victorian villa known as Oak View and it was being sold by F. Ashe Lincoln QC, a remarkable character who was a retired judge and a highly decorated Naval captain.

During the 1980s, I had established myself as a property developer and had created numerous homes by designing and converting old London houses into flats. I now had an opportunity to build my first new-build block of apartments.

Despite my seemingly successful business at the time, my living expenses were high and I had still not managed to amass any real capital. This development was potentially a game changer and all I needed was the finance.

My accountant friend, Henry, was prepared to put up the deposit to purchase the site on a 50/50 basis, the question then was to raise the rest of the purchase price.

An old friend of mine, Leon, together with his partner Hugh Taylor, had set up a contracting company under a government initiative called the 'Business Expansion Scheme'. Their BES company was prepared to fund the build cost of the development (ultimately amounting to around £2m), on the basis of taking a share of the profit on the deal.

On the back of that building contract commitment, I was able to borrow the site cost of £1m from the London branch of the American bank, Manufacturers Hanover Trust (which years later would morph into JP Morgan Chase).

Game on. I bought the site.

The projected gross value of the development was £5m which included a substantial inbuilt profit.

Although beautifully designed and approved by the local planning officers, the proposed development was a controversial project. We applied to the local authority to increase the density of the block from 14 to 18 flats.

In the 1980s, at a political level, broadly speaking the Conservative party tended to be pro-development and the Labour party anti-development, unless it was social housing.

Our application came before the local planning sub-committee, which was controlled by the Conservative party by one vote, assuming that the Liberal Democrats voted with Labour against the development.

At the crucial moment of the vote a Conservative councillor was called out of the chamber to attend a different committee and there was a stalemate.

I was in the public section and, unable to restrain myself, jumped out of my seat and started to berate the committee. At this point the political system in the

London Borough of Barnet broke down with most of the committee insisting that I did not have the right to speak, but in an ironic twist of fate the left wing and anti-development Labour Councillor, Frances Crook (later to be given the OBE for services to Penal Reform) said, and I paraphrase Voltaires' misattributed quote, "I disapprove of the development but defend Mr Lewis's right to speak."

This caused further pandemonium and the Conservative chairman, who was supportive of the development, ruled, "I abandon this sub-committee meeting in chaos, and refer the matter to the main Town Planning committee." Fortunately, the main committee was staunchly Conservative.

The *Hendon Times* was to report this event on their front page as, 'Local Developer causes chaos at the Town Hall.'

A few weeks later, at the main committee, I received the planning consent and by late 1986 we were on site starting the groundworks.

It would take two years to construct Oakview Lodge and by early 1988 we had completed 18 luxury apartments which stand out today as one of the finest residential developments in the local area. The actress Maureen Lipman topped out the block. We sold six apartments quite quickly at record prices.

It was now August 1988, and the Chancellor of the Exchequer, Nigel Lawson, decided to remove certain allowances under MIRAS (Mortgage Interest Relief at Source).

The market came to a dead halt for the next year. We still had 12 flats to sell and owed around £3m running up at 17% interest!

'THE MIRACLE OF OAKVIEW LODGE'

(Quote by Leon Glinsman)

We had renamed the building Oakview Lodge and although it consisted of 18 flats there were two entrances effectively dividing the property into two blocks of nine flats.

And so it was that in late 1989 our agent received a call from a Los Angeles broker who was in town and wanted to make an appointment for a client to see the remaining apartments. On the day of the appointment, a Mercedes minibus arrived and out stepped Princess Norhayati with her entourage. The Princess, who lived in a mansion in Winnington Road in Hampstead Garden Suburb, was the sister-in-law of the Sultan of Brunei and she was looking for some apartments for her staff.

She was interested in buying the nine apartments in Block A at the full asking price (£2.6m) but only if she could have them all. We were already under contract to sell one apartment in the block but felt confident that we could buy ourselves out of that commitment. However, of more concern was the fact that we had already completed the sale of a ground floor one bedroom apartment in Block A to the lovely Mrs Hyman, who was a widow of 88 years old.

Mrs Hyman had already furnished the apartment with beautiful fitted carpets, curtains and light fittings, and had already moved in. I went to see her and suggested that I was prepared to let her have a ground floor apartment in Block B in a free exchange. The new apartment was a two bedroom apartment and worth considerably more than her current unit.

Mrs Hyman had two sons who were keen for her to make the move as, by so, doing their inheritance would increase because they would have a bigger flat when she passed on, but not unreasonably they were concerned about placing too much pressure on her. I too, did not want the responsibility of causing her any distress.

Furthermore having furnished her home she was reluctant to move, but eventually on the strict understanding that I would furnish the new apartment with exactly the same carpet, curtains and fittings, and that I would replace every item in it's parallel position in the new apartment, she agreed. Readers may be amused at the idea that, on the day of the move, I could be seen on a stepladder inside the new flat adjusting the height of Mrs Hyman's curtains to ensure that she was happy.

We were accordingly able to deliver the nine apartments in Block A to the Princess with full vacant possession.

In a final twist, after completion, the Princess's solicitors telephoned me and asked me for all the keys to the block as the Princess needed full security. I said that they had keys to the nine leasehold apartments which they had purchased from me, but they had not purchased the freehold and they were not entitled to exclusive access to the entrance and common parts which I still controlled.

Oh, they said, but the Princess needs full security and therefore how much would it be to purchase the freehold?

At this point I explained that the freehold included the three vacant apartments in Block B and if they wanted to buy the freehold it would cost them £750,000.

OK, they said we will buy the freehold, and as a result, in late 1989, and in the face of a property market which had all but collapsed we had achieved the sale of the entire block.

I had given three years of my life to that project, with the very real prospect of a substantial profit from the project but it was not to be. I learned a lesson – timing is everything – but at least from a financial perspective we were saved by the miracle of the sale of Oakview Lodge to the Princess of Brunei.

(End - Volume 1)

Lightning Source UK Ltd.
Milton Keynes UK
UKHW011901280919
350609UK00008B/108/P